*The Irish National League in Dingle,
County Kerry, 1885–1892*

Maynooth Studies in Local History

SERIES EDITOR   Raymond Gillespie

This is one of the six titles to be published in the Maynooth Studies in Local History series in 2003. With these six the series will now comprise of over fifty volumes. The majority of these have their origins as theses completed for the M.A. in Local History course in NUI Maynooth that is itself ten years old. This achievement is evidence of the enthusiasm for the study of local history in Ireland but it also reflects the importance attached to local developments in the writing of the story of the Irish past in a new millennium. These volumes are also testimony to a growing methodological sophistication in the writing of Irish local history in the last ten years. Like many of their predecessors they employ the analytical framework of community in trying to understand local developments in the past. In a rapidly changing society 'community' has resonances of an idyllic society characterized by mutual support and a sense belonging held in tension with insularity and remoteness. As such the idea can conceal tensions and differences in such imagined worlds. Yet these local studies resist the tendency to such stereotyping. With their predecessors they reveal something of the realities of the workings of local communities in the changing world of the past. Individuals belonged to many communities in the past and such memberships were often fluid and determined by a variety of motives, agendas and external forces. Whether the community was that of the landed estate, local town, large city, political party or gentry world, its membership was continually fluctuating and those who belonged to these diverse communities were rarely of the same mind as each other. Social, religious and political divisions were all realities in these local worlds of the past, yet those who were often at odds with each other at least agreed on the basic rules for the debate, albeit sometimes the rules of violence or resistance. Countering the centrifugal forces often threatening to tear local societies apart, there were equally powerful centripetal tendencies holding it together. The way in which these forces combined created the local distinctiveness, or 'personality', of the local regions of Ireland. These studies, like their predecessors, contribute to an understanding of that process, and together they are remaking our understanding of modern Ireland.

Maynooth Studies in Local History: Number 48

The Irish National League in Dingle, County Kerry, 1885–1892

Donnacha Seán Lucey

FOUR COURTS PRESS

Set in 10pt on 12pt Bembo by
Carrigboy Typesetting Services, County Cork for
FOUR COURTS PRESS LTD
7 Malpas Street, Dublin 8, Ireland
e-mail: info@four-courts-press.ie
http://www.four-courts-press.ie
and in North America for
FOUR COURTS PRESS
c/o ISBS, 920 N.E. 58th Avenue, Suite 300, Portland, OR 97213.

© Donnacha Seán Lucey 2003

ISBN 1-85182-765-x

All rights reserved. Without limiting the rights under copyright reserved alone, no part of this publication may be reproduced, stored in or introduced into a retrieval system, or transmitted, in any form or by any means (electronic, mechanical, photocopying, recording or otherwise), without the prior written permission of both the copyright owner and the above publisher of this book.

Printed in Ireland by
ßetaprint Ltd, Dublin

Contents

	Acknowledgements	6
	Introduction	7
1	The establishment of the Irish National League in the Dingle area	13
2	The growth of the League	26
3	The decline and fall of the League	34
	Conclusion	54
	Notes	57

FIGURES

1	Map of the Dingle Peninsula	8
2	Burnham House, residence of Lord Ventry	15
3	Canon Dan O'Sullivan, founding member of the National League in Dingle	17
4	John Atkins Store, shop boycotted by the National League	23
5	Poster advertising a National League meeting in Dingle	39

TABLES

1	Number of land holdings and their size in statute acres in the Dingle poor law union	15
2	Number of agrarian outrages reported to the RIC between August 1885 and June 1886 in Co. Kerry and the Dingle RIC division	26
3	Number of boycotting cases reported to the RIC in County Kerry between October 1887 and March 1889	43

Acknowledgements

There are a number of people that I would like to thank for helping and assisting me during the course of my research. Firstly, I would like to thank all the teaching staff of the Department of History, NUI Maynooth, in particular Professor R.V. Comerford, Dr Raymond Gillespie and Dr Dympna McLoughlin. Also, I would like to acknowledge Dr Fergus Campbell, for his words of invaluable and indispensable advice.

I would like to thank all the staff of the following institutions and public repositories; John Paul II Library, NUI Maynooth, the National Archives of Ireland and the National Library of Ireland. Special mention is required for the staff of the Kerry County Library and particularly its excellent Local History section where Eamon Browne offered me his total assistance. Also I owe a depth of gratitude to the staff of the Dingle Library, particularly the head librarian, Cathy Murphy, for their help and use of their modern facilities and comprehensive collection of local history writings. I am also grateful to Tom Fox for the photographic images in this text.

I wish to extend particular thanks to Fr Jackie McKenna and Bernie Goggin for providing me with their unparalleled knowledge of the Dingle area; all my friends and past class-mates who assisted me in some way; last but not least my family, Sinead and Eileen my two sisters, Joan my mother and Eileen my aunt.

I wish to dedicate this book to the memory of my father.

Introduction

Dingle poor law union, an area more commonly known as West Kerry, is the focus of this study. It corresponds largely to the barony of Corkaguiny and the police division of Dingle. In 1876 the union comprised 125,279 acres (of which 93,629 acres were owned by Lord Ventry) and a further 11,531 acres of Lord Cork's Kerry property.[1] In the 1880s the area became embroiled in the political and social upheaval that engulfed most of the country. Central to this agitation was the role the Irish National League, a body founded in 1882, with the primary aim of achieving home rule. This work will tell the story of the dramatic rise and fall of the Irish National League in the region between 1885 and 1892 with much of the research focusing on the administrative, commercial and political centre of the union, Dingle town.

The land war that erupted on the western seaboard in 1879 was largely confined to Connacht. However, by the time the Land League was suppressed in 1881, Kerry had become one of the major centres of disturbances in the country. In 1879 only 13 agrarian crimes were committed in the county, but by the following year this had risen dramatically to 298. The majority of these occurred in the final three months of the year, a period that largely corresponded with the emergence of the Land League in the county.[2] Joseph Lee equates the rapid rise of Kerry to the forefront of the land agitation to demographic factors unique to the county. It witnessed a large increase in the number of unmarried men, similar to the situation experienced in the immediate post-Famine period in the rest of the country, who were willing to engage in the agrarian agitation. Lee also identifies the agricultural crisis created by the dramatic fall in the price of butter, a product many Kerry farmers were dependent on, as a reason for the eruption of the land war in the county.[3] However, there were other factors. Some of the largest estates in the country were located in Kerry and this, coupled with the presence of a notoriously harsh land agent, Edward Hussey, ensured that eviction campaigns were on a large scale, thus increasing tensions between landlords and tenants. Furthermore, some of the most effective Land League organizers of the period, notably Timothy and Edward Harrington, were the leading League figures in Kerry and they guaranteed the Land League agenda was forced to the forefront of society.

The Land League was originally established in the Dingle region in October 1880 following a series of evictions. The first League meeting, held on the burnt-out remains of an evicted house, prompted the spread of

1 Map of the Dingle Peninsula.

branches to Dingle and Castlegregory.[4] The region rapidly became embroiled in agrarian agitation. Although some violent outrages were committed, the Dingle region was not marked by the serious crime that characterized much of the county. In 1881, the government introduced coercive legislation that outlawed the Land League. In some parts of the country other organizations, such as the Ladies League, were established to replace the suppressed Land League branches, however these never emerged in the Dingle region. In 1882, the Irish National League was created with home rule at the centre of its agenda. Much continuity existed between the new organization and the Land League; their membership and branch structures were similar. However, whereas the Land League branches were semi-autonomous, the National League was hierarchically controlled, with power vested in the central branch located in Dublin and consisting of the leading members of the Irish Parliamentary Party, which had Charles Stuart Parnell as its president. The constitution of the National League declared that the attainment of parliamentary independence was its primary aim. The issues of land reform that motivated the Land League were relegated to secondary importance. Furthermore, the new organization proposed to act in a constitutional manner and therefore attempted to depart from the violence that often coexisted with the Land League.

Although the National League expanded rapidly in 1882 with over 200 branches established within three months of its inception,[5] the calming effect of the Crimes Act on the country and the languishing economic distress resulted in a period of relative inactivity in the League by 1883. The intensity of the agrarian agitation during this period also declined as indicated in the drop in the number of agrarian crimes committed. The change signalled what many contemporaries believed was the end of the first stage of the land war. Although 1884 remained relatively quite the National League's branch strength increased from 242 to 467 in the first six months of the year. Throughout the 1882–4 period there was a concerted effort by the National League leaders not to extend the organization to Kerry as they were wary that the violent nature of the county would undermine the League's constitutional attributes. However, by 1885, with the general election looming League organizers turned their attention to Kerry including the Dingle region: that is the point at which this book begins.

The sources on which this study is based are diverse. For any book examining a subject such as this, contemporary newspapers are of paramount importance. Thanks to the National school system that had been operating for half a century by 1881 illiteracy rates in Kerry had dropped significantly from 70 to 35 per cent as compared with 1841.[6] Thus, newspapers had potentially large readership rates and became a central medium for political activists. Like many other Irish counties, Kerry had two newspaper titles that diligently followed events on a local and national level with each representing one side of the political divide. The *Kerry Evening Post*, a paper that spanned three centuries (1774–1917), was unionist in outlook, while the *Kerry Sentinel* was in effect the mouthpiece of nationalism. The first edition of the *Kerry Sentinel* appeared on 26 April 1878 with Timothy Harrington as its creator and editor.[7] He had moved to Tralee from Castletownbere in Co. Cork to work in the town as a teacher. When the land war campaign in Kerry began in the latter half of 1880 Harrington became one of the Land League's leading organizers and his paper emerged as the League's voice in the county. In 1881 his brother, Edward Harrington, edited the paper while Timothy was imprisoned for Land League activity.[8] By 1885 Edward was the permanent editor of the paper and Timothy progressed as a leading figure nationally acting as an MP (Dublin Harbour) and secretary of the central branch of the League. In effect, the *Kerry Sentinel* became a propaganda machine for the National League. It provided detailed accounts of evictions, outrages, elections and the proceedings of the board of guardians – all cloaked in a nationalist viewpoint with the aim of demonizing the landlord class. Of importance to this study are the published reports of local National League meetings submitted to the newspaper by individual branches. Although these were undoubtedly censored either by the branches themselves or Edward Harrington, acting as editor, they offer an opportunity to document League activity. The *Kerry Evening Post,* for its part carried much of the same material but from the perspective of the landlords and the authorities. It regularly denounced the National League and actively reported on aspects of the agitation and league actions that the *Kerry Sentinel* ignored.

Police reports found in the Chief Secretary's Office Registered Papers (CSORP) located at the National Archives form another major source for this work. Although an extremely fragmented and difficult source to use, much information may be derived from these 'remarkable documents'.[9] The structure and layout of these reports were determined by the police administration of the time. The country was divided into four police divisions each with a divisional magistrate (these divisional magistrates replaced the special resident magistrates in 1883).[10] Dublin Castle received monthly reports from the various magistrates on the state of the country which in turn determined much of the chief secretary's policy. These reports were based on the various county inspectors' reports within the division, whose report was in turn compiled from the district inspectors' reports from around the county. The county report made a general comment on the area and then provided two or three of the district inspector's reports from the most disturbed areas. So, in the case of Dingle, either a remark made by the county inspector for the Dingle district or the full report from the district inspector may be found in the divisional magistrates monthly report to the chief secretary. Based on intelligence gathered by the constabulary at a local level, they are a rich source of information on the rise of the National League, the amount of boycotting and agrarian outrages and the general attitude of the police. From August 1886 these monthly reports are no longer found in the CSORP but in the Irish National League Papers, also located in the National Archives. While this source is indispensable, it is very incomplete. Many documents are missing from the collection, largely attributable to the fire at the Four Courts in 1922.

The personal papers of Timothy Harrington held in the National Library of Ireland form another source that facilitated this research. All manner of papers relating to both Land and National League activity feature in this collection. The most valuable to this topic include a series of letters from the secretaries of local National League branches in the Dingle region to Harrington acting in his capacity as the national secretary of the League. The corresponding letters from Harrington are found in the manuscript 'National League Letter Book 1883–86', in the National Library of Ireland.[11] These two sets of letters yield much information on the inner workings of the National League in the Dingle area. They offer an insight into the local dynamics behind many of the National League actions while also providing an opportunity to analyse the national leadership's policy towards individual branches.

Contemporary directories including *Slater's directory for 1881* and *Guy's Munster directory for 1886* provide information on the various towns and villages located in the Dingle region. Data concerning each area's size, population and commercial assets are provided. Also, the name of each shopkeeper, trader, publican and other persons of note is listed, as are the local gentry and clergy.

Furthermore, a small number of strong farmers are named, although their acreage is not provided. These sources were particularly useful for analysing the social background of the leading figures that emerged during the agitation.

Parliamentary papers also provided a significant amount of material for this work. The government published annual returns concerning evictions and outrages. These offer the opportunity to chart the intensity of the agitation but the data is only provided by county and not by police district. This problem was overcome, particularly in relation to agrarian crime, by utilizing the information in the police reports offering the opportunity to compare local and county levels of crime. Also, there is a wide range of material published in the parliamentary papers concerning the administration of each poor law union in the country. Reports of various government commissions relevant to the period are also located in the parliamentary papers. In the *Report of the royal commission on the Land Law (Ireland) Act, 1881, and Purchase of Land (Ireland) Act, 1885* (more commonly known as the Cowper Commission), statements were made in relation to the effects of boycotting in the Dingle area.[12] Furthermore, the establishment of the Special Commission in 1888 after the infamous Pigott letters, led to prosecuting lawyers calling up witnesses from all around the country. In their attempt to associate the National League with agrarian crime and outrage Kerry became central to the prosecution's case. Consequently, a number of witnesses from the Dingle region gave evidence in relation to the National League in the Dingle area. The minutes of this commission were published separately from the parliamentary papers as *Special Commission Act, 1888: reprint of the shorthand notes of the speeches, proceedings and evidence taken before the commissioners appointed under the above act* (London, 1890).

A definitive history of the National League or the land war in general in either Co. Kerry as a whole or in the Dingle region remains to be completed. Arguably the leading work on the National League in Dingle remains Patrick Foley's *A history of the natural, civil, military and ecclesiastical state of county Kerry: Corkaguiny*. Foley's work was published in 1907 and gives an extremely nationalist account of the events that marked the period. Although at times it is difficult to determine what sources he used, the *Kerry Sentinel* is often quoted along with information from parliamentary papers. Furthermore, considering the time proximity to the events it describes, it may be presumed that much of his information was acquired from first hand accounts. Although a product of its time, Foley's account proved indispensable as a reference point in the course of this study. Arguably the last attempt to write a general history of the Dingle region came from Thomas O'Sullivan's, *Romantic hidden Kerry*.[13] While the work is an extremely detailed and comprehensive account of Dingle's past, the section on the National League is largely a reproduction of Foley's writings, although extra information from parliamentary papers is included.

Modern scholarship on the National League in the Dingle region is non-existent. However, much research has been undertaken on the period from the mid to late 1880s on a national scale. Margaret O'Callaghan's *British high politics and a nationalist Ireland*, examines the British response to Irish nationalism and argues that conservative policy successfully criminalized the home rule movement through the rigorous examination of individual actions of local branches of the National League in the Special Commission of 1888.[14] Donald Jordan's article 'The Irish National League and the "unwritten law": rural protest and nation building in Ireland 1882–90' attempts to examine the National League on a local basis.[15] He writes of an 'unwritten law' that he traces back to James Fintan Lalor where tenants believed they had a right to only pay what rent they could. Jordan argues that this formed the basis of the law of the 'league courts' that followed. Also, the National League's relationship with boycotting and agrarian outrages is examined. However, O'Callaghan and Jordan largely fail to evaluate features of National League activity, such as the role of non-tenants in the movement, like agricultural labourers. Nor do these works document any of the tensions that prevailed in the movement locally. The work of J.S. Donnelly Jnr is a prerequisite for any examination of National League activity on a local level. His *Land and the people of nineteenth-century Cork* and more relevant to this work, 'The Kenmare estates in the nineteenth century' document some National League activity in these areas.[16] Nevertheless, these works are primarily based on estate papers, and little attention is given to National League sources such as the Harrington papers or police reports. Hence, at times Donnelly's work largely concentrates on estate management and doesn't provide a full-blown account of the National League.

The major published work in relation to the poor law unions and the involvement of the Land and National League activists in them, remains William Feingold's *The revolt of the tenantry: the transformation of local government in Ireland, 1872–86*.[17] In this work Feingold highlights the involvement of local League branches in the poor law unions and the transfer of power that occurred on the board of guardians (also known as poor law boards) from landlords to tenants. However, as Virginia Crossman has commented, Feingold's 'analysis inevitably oversimplifies a complex procedure'.[18] Feingold also fails to document the role of the union's controlling body, the Local Government Board, in controlling League-dominated poor law boards. In examining the National League's actions within the Dingle poor law union and on the board of guardians this research augments the current material while also offering new insights into the topic.

1. The establishment of the Irish National League in the Dingle area

Situated on the Dingle peninsula in the south-west of Ireland the various regions within the Dingle poor law union were intertwined politically, socially, administratively and commercially. By the emergence of the land war in 1880, the poor law union had become the principal unit of local government in Ireland. Although, initially established under the 1838 Poor Law Act to combat poverty through the workhouse system, its importance grew as it created the basic structure upon which a social service system evolved. Under the Medical Charities Act of 1851 the responsibilities of the boards were expanded, providing not only poor relief but also medical care and health services generally. Unions were divided into dispensary districts, each with a qualified medical officer providing home relief, while workhouses were opened not just to the destitute but also the widespread sick.[1] Other duties imposed on the boards included diverse responsibilities such as the maintenance of proper drainage, sewerage, burial grounds, registration of voters and marriages, food and workshop inspection, vaccination, and the fostering out and education of orphaned children. Furthermore, a host of employees were under the control of the union including workhouse masters, doctors, nurses, cooks, teachers, inspectors and clerks of various kinds. Its patronage extended to the giving out of contracts for food, fuel, medicines and public work projects.[2] In effect, the poor law unions were the primary local government bodies of the time and wielded a considerable amount of power.

The unions were administered by poor law boards, which were also known as 'boards of guardians'. These were composed of elected and appointed guardians. Elected guardians (usually tenants from the local community) served alongside local magistrates (invariably the local landlords) who acted as ex-officio guardians, in a ratio of three-quarters elected to one-quarter ex-officio.[3] Qualification for election depended on the value of the land an individual owned or rented. By 1886, the average qualification required for election to the board of guardians was a land valuation of at least £20, although this figure varied as the rate could be set by the individual board of guardians or the local government board.[4] Similarly, voting rights were based on property status as occupiers and owners of land received a number of votes from a scale of one to six depending on the value of their land which in turn decided the amount of rates they paid to the union.[5] Undoubtedly the poor law union system of government was the most democratic government

13

institution in Ireland with over 500,000 people qualified to vote[6] and was the only administrative body in rural areas with directly elected representatives. It offered the Catholic middle classes a degree of power since since membership of the boards provided access to decision-making processes as well as a significant source of patronage. Yet it maintained and protected the propertied classes through the system of voting and appointment of ex-officio members. Furthermore, the non-propertied members of the board were usually tenants of the ex-officio appointees; thus ensuring the balance of power was tipped in the favour of the landed class. Research undertaken by William Feingold has demonstrated that the landlord class had dominated the unions and boards of guardians before the land war. He calculated that of the controlling positions of the board of guardians (chairman, vice-chairman and deputy vice-chairman), 93 per cent were held by landowners in 1877.[7] The situation on the Dingle boards of guardians was no different from the national picture. The largest landowner in the union, Lord Ventry, held the most powerful position on the board (chairman), while his land agent and brother was vice-chairman. However, tenants far outnumbered landowners and could depose their landlords so long as they voted together.

Poor law unions varied in size and population right across the country with the largest being Glenties union in Donegal with an area of 257,479 acres and the smallest in the North Dublin union with 41,256.[8] The Dingle poor law union roughly equalled the national average with 125,279 acres while its population in 1881 amounted to 20,142. Administratively the union was divided into electoral divisions, dispensary districts and registrar divisions. There were 19 electoral divisions that provided 21 guardians. For the purpose of the general registration of births and deaths and the dispensary system, the union was divided into four districts comprised of the various electoral divisions. The area with the highest population density was the Dingle register district with 5,775 people residing it. The largest urban centre within that area and the union as a whole was Dingle town with a population in 1881 of 1,833.[9] The principles governing the formation of each union originally was to 'fix upon some market town conveniently situated as a centre and to attach to it the whole surrounding district of which it may be considered the capital'.[10] Population-wise, Dingle town was the obvious candidate to act as the union's 'capital'. Furthermore, it was centrally connected to the various regions within the union by road. Also, Dingle was the commercial heart of the union, having an active harbour with weekly steamer sailings to and from Cork and being the location of monthly fairs. Although, by the time of the emergence of the National League in 1885 neither the town nor the union in general was connected by railway, there was a daily car service to Tralee.[11] Acting as the centre of the union and the region in general, Dingle town provided much of the impetus behind the agitation of the period.

The establishment of the Irish National League in the Dingle area

2 Burnham house, residence of Lord Ventry.

Lord Ventry's estate of 93,629 acres made up much of the 125,278 acres situated in the union. The other prominent property owner in the area was an absentee landlord, the earl of Cork and Orrery, who possessed 11,531 acres in the union.[12] According to the census of 1881, the 125,278 acres of the union was divided into 2,201 individual holdings ranging from a plot of land under one acre to over 500 acres.[13] Table 1 depicts the distribution in size of those holdings in the Dingle poor law union for the year 1881.

Table 1. Number of land holdings and their size in statute acres in the Dingle poor law union

Acres	0–1	2–5	6–15	16–20	21–50	51–100	101–200	201–500	+501
Number	113	166	330	516	449	399	159	58	11

Source: *Return of the agricultural statistics for the year 1881*, p. 19.

The union was dominated by pasture farming with 69,403 acres under grass, while only 11,573 acres were used for growing crops. Of these crops, potatoes were the most popular, with over 19,000 tonnes produced in 1881. To a lesser extent crops such as oats, wheat and barley along with turnips and hay featured in the agricultural output of the union.¹⁴ A significant 30,885 acres of the union was listed as barren mountain land, and a further 8,336 acres were designated as marsh and bog, indicating the infertile and unproductive nature of much of the land.¹⁵

In 1885 the Irish National League established itself in Dingle. Unlike the Land League of the 1879–82 period the National League's primary concern was not agrarian but political. This transformation occurred between the years 1882 and 1885 which witnessed the politicization of the Irish Parliamentary Party, as the party's leaders endeavoured to distance themselves from violent agrarian issues and forge a constitutional political identity, committed to the achievement of home rule.¹⁶ Although in existence since 1882, the National League's potential strength was not capitalized on in Kerry. Yet, by 1885 with the upcoming general election Charles Stewart Parnell and his lieutenants set about enhancing the position of the National League in order to increase support for home rule and provide the necessary local organization for the successful return of nationalist candidates. This new initiative from the national leadership, coincided with the looming agricultural depression created after increased international competition resulted in butter prices falling drastically.¹⁷ This increased anxiety among the tenantry and led to the rapid growth of the National League throughout the country. At the beginning of 1885 there were only nine branches in existence in Kerry but by July this had risen to 23 while at the end of the year there were 50 branches in the county (nationally the figure rose to 1,285).¹⁸ Dingle and its surrounding hinterland were to be engulfed in this massive increase in National League activity, leading to profound effects on the local political landscape.

Like many instances all over the country the National League became established in Dingle after a public meeting was held in the town. This took place on 5 May 1885 and was addressed by the leading National League advocates in the county along with local figures. The most prominent speaker was Edward Harrington, president of the Tralee National League and brother of the secretary of the central branch and national leader Timothy Harrington MP. Edward Harrington was also the proprietor of the League mouthpiece, and pro-nationalist paper in the county, *The Kerry Sentinel*. In his speech to the Dingle audience, the aims and objectives of the National League were clearly stated: 'one is national self government, second is to obtain land reform and third is to obtain local self government and the extension of the franchise'.¹⁹ Here we see the transformation of the National League from a purely agrarian organization such as the Land League to the establishment of a broader agenda with the attainment of home rule as its prime objective. According to Harrington, a 'league of Irishmen' was to be created whose 'ranks shall comprise of everyone who can pretend to the name of Irishman, the farmer, the labourer, the artisan, the shopkeeper, the trader, the sailor'.²⁰ Such a

The establishment of the Irish National League in the Dingle area

3 Canon Dan O'Sullivan, founding National League member in Dingle.

statement illustrates the cross section of society to which the National League was appealing to under the umbrella of nationalism. Despite this, Harrington, realizing the political reality of the time and the importance of the support of farmers if the National League was to succeed, stated that

> as this county is principally a county of agricultural industry we seek the advancement of tenant farmers. We are to a certain extent more wedded to him than to any other individual in the country.[21]

Such a strong acknowledgement of farmers indicates Harrington's awareness that despite the home rule aspirations of the national leadership agrarian issues were to remain a fundamental element of the new League's policy in the Dingle region. Local personalities that were present on the platform and who came to form the leadership of the National League in Dingle were representative of the strong middle class of farmer and trader who were dominant in the earlier Land League. The principal local speaker was Michael Dissette, a publican in the town; and other figures such as John Lee, a hotel owner, and Thomas Kelliher, a prominent farmer were also present as were the clergy with the local parish priest Canon Dan O'Sullivan acting as chairman.[22]

While the leading figures of the Irish Parliamentary Party may have successfully converted their political ideology from agrarian concerns to the attainment of home rule, doubts must arise how much these local figures, who were in place from the Land League, had revolutionized their aspirations and were willing to sideline agrarian issues.

The National League as a whole, with its primary aim of promoting home rule, was anxious to emphasize its political status. Unlike the semi-autonomous Land League, Parnell and the inner circle of the Irish Parliamentary Party effectively controlled the organisation. In theory, the National League was to be run by a council where the Parliamentary Party would have the nomination of 16 members out of a council of 42 while the remaining 32 would be elected by the county conventions composed of delegates from the individual branches. In practice this never transpired, as power was transferred to the temporary central branch that remained in place for the duration of the organization's existence. Although it gave the impression of a far-sighted democratic organization, it was effectively an over-centralized hierarchical body[23] with control vested in the central branch composed of elected MPs who had the power to overturn individual branches' decisions. Notwithstanding its autocratic nature, the League flourished, and no more so than in the Dingle area. Soon after the initial National League meeting in Dingle, a branch was created.[24] By September it was reported that large numbers had enrolled.[25] Another branch on the western side of Dingle was formed in Ballyferriter, while October saw the establishment of the Castlegregory league. Camp and Annascaul were added to the list leading to five active National League branches in the area encompassed by the Dingle poor law union by the general election in December 1885.[26]

A number of reasons explain this rapid rise in the number of branches. First, the new initiative of the national leadership provided the necessary support while also instilling the idea of nationalism into the public consciousness. This was fuelled by the rigorous campaigning of organizers, such as Edward Harrington, at numerous public meetings held in the county. The nationalist press in the form of the *Kerry Sentinel* disseminated the ideas of the movement and thereby increased its popularity. In Dingle itself, a politicized middle class composed of an economically interdependent alliance of traders and farmers with clerical backing was in place to provide the leadership. The agricultural depression was already affecting the tenant population: Lord Ventry had already enforced evictions on his estate the month before to the National League's establishment in Dingle. Although according to the parish priest in Dingle they were 'perfectly justified as they only took place where there were 5 or 6 years rent due', the *Kerry Sentinel* portrayed them as another case of unjust evictions.[27] The situation worsened with the prosecution of four tenants for retaking their holdings after having been evicted on that occasion.

Arguably the most impressive aspect of the National League as an organization was its effectiveness as a political machine and its canvassing of voters for the Irish Parliamentary Party. Under the rules of the League, each branch sent a delegation of its members to a county convention for the purpose of electing candidates to run during elections; the process was seemingly embedded in democratic principles, as candidates were decided first by votes at local branch and then by votes at the county convention. The localized nature of the proceedings was intended to guarantee the involvement of all members from grassroots level. At the country convention held in Tralee in November, just before the general election, the Dingle League was represented by John Lee, Michael Dissette, Michael McDonnell and Thomas Kelliher.[28] Lee was a hotel owner, Dissette a publican and the latter two were prominent farmers – all indicators of the strong middle-class leadership of the National League;[29] the branch also nominated 'Mr M.D. Kavanagh as a fit and proper representative for parliament' for the West Kerry seat.[30] The local Christian Brothers School was made available to the National League for the convention. Of the 277 delegates that attended, 60, or almost a fifth, were clergy – an indication of the level of support that the church provided for the National League. During the meeting, which was held behind closed doors, Kavanagh, the Dingle candidate, did not offer his nomination, and Edward Harrington was selected as the candidate for West Kerry.[31] The *Kerry Sentinel* reported that the event passed off with 'the entire absence on anything approaching dissension in the slightest degree',[32] but it is highly probable that Harrington received support from the central branch which ensured his victory. The previous August, Harrington was ousted from his position as president of the Tralee National League for his failure to meet demands to stop publishing non-GAA sports reports in his paper, the *Kerry Sentinel*.[33] Thanks to his strong personal ties with the central branch (his brother Timothy was secretary), the decision was overturned; the *Sentinel* continued to carry reports on sports such as cricket and rugby.[34] Similarly, it was rumoured that Harrington was put in place for the West Kerry seat by the Parliamentary Party – illustrating that despite the democratic appearance of the National League, power was vested in the hierarchical authority of central branch.[35] However, unlike the infamous instance in Galway, where Parnell forced the candidacy of Captain O'Shea on a non-welcoming tenantry, leading to what became known as the 'Galway Mutiny', little acrimony seemed to exist after the failure of the Dingle nomination. The Dingle branch passed a resolution endorsing Harrington, often which the candidate gave a pre-election speech in the town which, he claimed, was 'met with great enthusiasm'[36]. Polling day witnessed such a huge turnout in Dingle that a second polling booth was needed but the authorities declined to provide one – which meant that many were unable to vote. Notwithstanding this, Harrington easily beat the Conservative challenge from William Rowen, a

Tralee landlord, by 2,607 to 202;[37] and National League candidates captured the other three seats in Kerry along with the vast majority in Ireland outside the unionist north. The general election victory gave Parnell his strongest hand ever in the house of commons and pushed the home rule issue to the forefront of British politics. Much of this success may be attributed to the smooth running of the National League electioneering machinery, which had hitherto been lacking in the Parliamentary Party. It not only galvanized a strong vote but also removed the selection of candidates from the hands of meetings and local clubs to the county conventions where the party and Parnell could have a direct influence over events. The massive success of nationalist candidates not only illustrated that the National League was an extremely efficient and extensive infrastructure of the organization but also demonstrated its wish to act constitutionally. However, it would be wrong to read the National League's role in the election as entirely democratic, for power over decision-making, particularly in relation to the selection of candidates, was in the control of central branch who could veto the power of individual branches.

While the branches of the National League provided the infrastructure for the nationalist success in the general election, their most dramatic effect was to be found on the ground, where they began to tackle the political and social dominance of landlordism. Although the League's primary concern was the attainment of home rule, the driving force behind local politics remained agrarian. With the establishment of the National League it was inevitable that the organization would openly oppose evictions. The eviction process underlined the authority of landlordism and served as a reminder or a threat to the tenant population of the result of non-payment of rent. In most instances landlords readmitted evicted tenants as caretakers, but a full eviction, where the occupant was ejected from the land, left a farm unoccupied. That farm would then be reallocated to other tenant who would be more liable to pay his rent. (When a full eviction took place, any produce remaining on the farm such as livestock or hay could be sold to recoup the landlord's losses). It was in this area that the National League most actively tackled landlordism; it sought to make evictions an unviable option for landlords by preventing other farmers from taking evicted farms. To prevent such 'land grabbing', the most powerful weapon that was at the disposal of the League was the 'boycott'. While the boycott was used as a weapon targeted at landlords, it also gave the League unique power to enforce and exercise its control over the community at large.

Campaigns of social and economic ostracism had long been a form of peasant agitation, particularly during the land war, where it acquired the name of 'boycotting'. On the eve of the establishment of the National League, some boycotting was already in existence in Dingle, mainly aimed at eviction parties in the town, on one occasion 'bailiffs who accompanied Lord Vent couldn't obtain food for love or money or shelter'.[38] Yet, it was ... League that would capitalise fully on its potential strength. The methods be... a boycott were fully described to the audience who had congregated to witness the initial League meeting in Dingle as, 'if any man should take a [evicted] farm, it will be looked upon as a land cursed ...; avoid a man that would do so like a plague, look upon him as socially excommunicated'.[39] While the National League policy was to restrict boycotting to 'land grabbers', the national leadership often forcibly discouraged its use altogether. Writing to a Co. Cork branch, Timothy Harrington said, 'Any advice I would give to you would be rather in the direction of condemning the practice of boycotting as largely I could'.[40] However, boycotting was to become a central aspect of National League activity as it became the principal weapon of the League.

Breach of League rules in relation to 'land grabbing' and the subsequent administration of boycotts were dealt with through the weekly branch meetings. As the League attempted to enforce its edicts, these meetings became saturated with cases and rapidly came to resemble 'courts' – so much so that the RIC the district inspector for the Dingle area, Alexander Gray, claimed that the National League 'is nothing more than a court of inquiry for offences against its own laws'.[41] These 'League courts' adopted the forms, methods and language of legal tribunals. Significantly, in doing so they did not offer a radical alternative to the existing law institutions of the petty sessions but closely modelled themselves on the established forms.[42] Similar to the Land League courts of the earlier agitation, these National League courts comprised members of the local branch committee who summoned defendants and witnesses, heard cases, considered evidence, issued judgments and assigned penalties.[43] Proceedings were begun in these cases with complaints being raised orally against an individual or business organization by a branch member at a meeting. Offences ranged from 'land grabbing' and grazing on evicted farms to holding any form of contact with a boycotted person, either economically or socially. Cases were usually heard at the following branch meeting where the defendant could contest the charges and the committee hand down its verdict. If the offender offered an apology to the League and ceased the offensive behaviour, he or she was usually acquitted. However, failure to apologize so often led to condemnation of the person, while non-attendance led to the case being heard *in absentia* – with invariably the same outcome. Individual branches could refer cases to the Central Branch of the National League, which it also acted as a court of appeal and had the power to overturn branch decisions.[44]

An instance of one National League meeting of the Dingle branch during September 1885 will show how these courts actually worked. Several charges were issued against four shopkeepers for selling to 'landlord's men' and the four were promptly summoned to appear before the League to explain their actions. In another case, a carman who was ordered to appear at the previous meeting on a complaint of working for Lord Ventry offered an apology for his actions and pleaded that 'he would rather go to the workhouse than to work for him', thus avoiding punishment.[45] On another occasion at a Ballyferriter branch meeting, a farmer sent a letter claiming he would no longer occupy an evicted farm. Unsure of the correct procedure, the committee referred the issue to the central branch.[46] This sort of activity dominated League meetings throughout the area as the League began to create an alternative legal system to that of the crown. Although National League meetings were held on private property and admitted no strangers, the proceedings of its courts were widely publicized. In Castlegregory, lists of names were put on walls of the League rooms, and after the meeting a public announcement in the village was made of who was condemned.[47] The *Kerry Sentinel* constantly carried reports of League meetings, detailing the cases heard; these were positioned alongside reports of petty session hearings a suggestion that they were at least on a par with the established courts. Officially, the national leadership of the League claimed that the proceedings at branch meetings were no different from those of tenant right associations or trade unions – that they settled only minor arguments that were in the past dealt with by the local priest, and therefore helped to maintain social order in Ireland.[48] However, failure to comply with the League's rulings led to punishments in the form boycotting (other sentences imposed by the League included expulsion and fines), thus giving it a far greater significance.

Due to the rigour with which the National League carried out its boycotts, the process was having a significant effect on the intended targets. On one occasion, a process server who issued three writs for eviction on National League members reported how he couldn't get 'milk and potatoes and butter and anything else'.[49] The case of William Collier demonstrates the strength and effectiveness of boycotting in the Dingle area. Described as 'gentry' under *Guy's postal directory for Munster 1886*, he leased large tracts of land from local landowners.[50] He was originally boycotted for dealing with Atkins & Co., a condemned shopkeeper, because 'on principle [he] refused to join in the annoyance of this house and continued to deal with them',[51] thus offering clear resistance to the National League. Although the original shopkeeper came to a peace with the League, the boycott on Collier's continued as the branch claimed that he was 'Sam Hussey's [local landlord] agent and factotum in Dingle',[52] while Collier maintained he was being boycotted simply for disobeying the League.[53] The boycott against Collier illustrates the extent to which the method could paralysze its targets. Anyone connected with him received the same treatment so that 'his son, son in law and servant were unable to buy bread'.[54] Ordinary supplies were unattainable

4 Atkins store on Main St, Dingle. Boycotted for breaking National League rules.

in the town and had to be shipped in from Liverpool and Cork. To get his horse shod, he had to drive into Tralee, a distance of 32 miles.[55] Although many labourers were in a distressed state at the time, he could not acquire the services of any. When Collier successfully managed to employ some, 'the League boycotted these men and said if they did not at once leave the employment they would not get any supplies'; they capitulated.[56] The vigour and extent to which this boycott was carried out depicts the effectiveness of the method. The boycott on Collier handicapped his life and business interests, but he did have the means to withstand it (it lasted at least a year).[57]

Those who were not in such a fortunate situation could not do so. Support for the League outside the landlord class was not universal, even among the traders of the town. Four shopkeepers were called in front of the League for breaking its rules by serving emergency men.[58] The boycott on the Atkins & Co. emerged after it continued to serve bailiffs, police and emergency men. The shop was forced to take the drastic measures of reducing its prices to half the ordinary rate in an attempt to encourage trade.[59] All the boycotted parties eventually settled their differences with the League: boycotting had become such 'a powerful weapon to threaten with as it means ruination to the person on whom it is visited and consequently most people prefer to fall in line with the League'.[60]

Very few had the ability to resist a boycott, and many of those who did eventually caved in. Mr John Mason, a farmer who grazed on evicted land, was 'not only boycotted but nobody was to hold any conversation with him; ... he humbly gave up the land and apologized' and stated that 'he would have no more to do with the evicted farm'.[61] On another occasion, Mr Watson, a local farmer, was reported to the League for entering a shop whose owner was being boycotted; he now was unable to find anyone to shoe his horse, so that he was 'compelled before them [the League] to say I'm sorry gentleman for what I have done but if you overlook my fault this time I promise not to err for the future'.[62] Through the use of boycotting the League had created a position in which it had become the most powerful organization or institution in the locality. District Inspector Alexander Gray wrote that by the beginning of 1886 the 'prominent authority at present is the League'.[63] Within a couple of months he was of the opinion that 'the law of the land is nowhere and the law of the League everywhere.'[64]

Resolutions passed at National League meetings, particularly those that initiated boycotts, were often forwarded to other branches to increase the geographical area of the boycott and enhance its effectiveness. As already noted, William Collier had to travel a distance of over 30 miles to get his horse shod, and he had to source all his supplies outside the county. In another instance, 'Mr John Teahon a cattle dealer ... came to the attention of the League for selling cattle to the Land Corporation [an organization set up by landlords in 1880 to combat the effects of boycotting]' in Tralee.[65] Before he was to have his case heard he attended the Dingle fair, which he 'believed was his stronghold and having numerous friends and relatives there ... consequently he went to buy as usual but up to the hour of 11 p.m. he succeeded in buying only one solitary beast'.[66] This example indicates that the League's extensive branch network were regularly in contact thus strengthening the scope and reach of boycotts and maximising their effect.

By the start of 1886, the National League had proved itself a powerful organization. In providing Parnell with the general election success of

December it demonstrated extraordinary capabilities as an electoral machine. Local branches were fundamental to this success through the mobilization of voters and selection of candidates. The process of the county convention was a stroke of genius by Parnell as it gave the impression of a system where all members from the lowest level had an influence on proceedings. In reality, it provided the Parliamentary Party with the ability to maintain direct control over the selection process of candidates. However, despite the emergence of home rule as the primary aim of the party, the objectives of local National League branches remained agrarian. Local branches paid lip service to home rule and played their assigned roles at election time, yet it was agrarian issues such as evictions and the improvement of the living conditions of the tenantry that drove the League locally.

2. The growth of the League

Unlike previous agrarian movements such as the Whiteboys and Ribbonmen, the National League was not a secret society. Its proceedings and judgments were carried out in full public view through the medium of the press, word of mouth and public announcements. It made every effort 'to operate not outside the law as such, but merely outside the corrupt laws of a distant and questionable authority'[1] and tried to distance itself from the violence that marked the earlier Land League period. The national leadership of the League, in the form of the secretary of the central branch, constantly warned branches not to resort to violence as the Irish Parliamentary Party endeavoured to maintain its constitutional political identity committed to home rule. However, as the National League developed its extensive network of branches countrywide, resulting in a renewal of agrarian agitation fought through the 'League courts' and subsequent boycotting, the incidence of agrarian crime rose. The failure to renew the Crimes Act (*habeas corpus* was restored in the first half of 1885)[2] and the impact of the agricultural depression were significant factors in causing the rise in agrarian crime; but contemporaries tended to attribute this increase to the expansion of the National League. The county inspector of Kerry commented that 'in this county of Kerry ... it is a remarkable fact that the districts in which there are no branches the record of crime is practically nil'.[3]

During the 1880s Kerry had reached a degree of notoriety for its violent conduct that was unparalleled for any other county in the country. When the Special Commission was established in 1888, the case of Kerry was vital for the prosecution as in its attempt in its to portray the Irish Land and National Leagues as criminal conspiracies that organized and orchestrated agrarian crime.[4] The police returns for a ten-month period between August 1885 and June 1886 show the lawlessness into which the county had descended.

Table 2. Number of agrarian outrages reported to the RIC between August 1885 and June 1886 in Co. Kerry and the Dingle RIC Division

Month	Aug.	Sept.	Oct.	Nov.	Dec.	Jan.	Feb.	Mar.	Apr.	May	Jun.
County Kerry	25	16	27	22	14	11	17	17	28	21	31
Dingle RIC Division	0	1	2	1	1	1	1	0	1	3	2

Source: these figures are based on a combination of the NAI CSORP 1886, box 3302/1887 and crimes listed in Thomas O'Sullivan, *Romantic hidden Kerry: a description of Corkaguiny* (Tralee, 1931), pp 246–79.

Serious crimes such as murder, attempted murder and firing at the person were commonplace. For example, the returns for June 1886, one of the most violent months, show that in the Killarney district a 63-year-old named Patrick Tagney who worked for a landlord was killed, and in Tralee an Edward Herbert who grazed an evicted farm was shot at and wounded.[5] Less serious agrarian crimes such as intimidation, threatening letters and the killing and maiming of cattle were common in many parts of Kerry. Yet, much of this crime was concentrated in a triangular area marked by the three main towns of the county – Tralee, Killarney and Listowel. Interestingly, the Dingle area failed to become embroiled in the violence that engulfed much of the county. The district inspector for Dingle, Gray, remarked in January 1886, that 'compared with other districts in the county this shows a relatively clean sheet'.[6] He contended that even though 'Dingle was perhaps the most active centre for boycotting in this county ... outrages of a very serious nature are becoming very rare'.[7] Notwithstanding this, he did equate the rise in agrarian crime with the National League. He was of the opinion that 'there has been more outrages since the first branch was established in May last than there were for at least two years previous'.[8] Minor crimes did occur, but these were, in the words of the RIC sergeant for Annascaul, Andrew Shea, merely the 'maiming of cattle ... nothing more serious than that'.[9]

Where agrarian crimes occurred, they seem to have co-existed with National League activity. Without question, the most serious local outrage in the period was an attack on a man named Giles Rae (from Killiney) in Castlegregory. Gray described the crime as follows:

> On the 30th [January 1886] a party of five or six men with blackened faces entered the house of Giles Rae, a process server [of eviction notices] in Dingle District; four of them seized him and one caught his right ear which he sliced off with a razor, at the same time inflicting a deep gash on his neck.[10]

Rae, who was 74 years of age, had been boycotted previously for serving writs for eviction on four members of the National League, after which he claimed he couldn't get 'milk, potatoes, butter and anything else';[11] just before his attack he served another writ on a League member, Thomas O'Connor. After this particularly vicious assault, he remained boycotted in the Dingle and Castlegregory regions.[12] It is difficult to ascertain to what extent the National League orchestrated the outrage. Whatever the circumstances around the attack, it was unusual for the area and largely contradicted the League's official policy towards agrarian crime. Branch resolutions regularly denounced such actions. The Ballyferriter League declared that they 'condemn and reprobate all outrages and urge branches of all the National League in those districts (where crime occurred) [to] exert their whole influence against the commission of those dastardly acts',[13] while the Ventry branch pledged 'to say and do nothing which would be considered illegal'.[14] In articles and editorials, the National League's mouthpiece, the *Kerry Sentinel*, regularly distanced the movement from agrarian crime. On one occasion it argued that 'the greater number of moonlighting outrages are committed by unemployed labourers and young sons indicating that they are not wholly due to agrarian causes ... are only moonlight robberies and mischievous freaks of unemployed labourers'.[15] Although such proclamations can be seen as propaganda they also illustrate the National League's determination to distance itself from agrarian violence. While arguably there was a correlation between the National League activity and serious agrarian crime in some parts of the county, this situation did not appear to emerge in the Dingle region as the instance of outrage remained low. In fact, considering the dominant position of the League on the Dingle peninsula through its court system and successful implementation of boycotting campaigns, one could argue that the League's judicial activities substantially curtailed the resort to agrarian violence.[16]

As noted in the previous chapter, a central aspect of National League activity was the targeting of the process of evictions by boycotting, particularly against 'land grabbers' (tenants who took evicted farms). This not only offered tenants a degree of security but it also provided the League with a means to challenge landlord authority. The League also attempted to regulate other aspects of landlord-tenant relations. It often set the standard of rent that should be paid, usually at either Grittith's valuation or a 20–40 per cent reduction of the existing rent, as had been the case during the first stage of the land war.[17] From the evidence available, it is difficult to determine whether there was a concerted effort by the National League in the Dingle region to achieve such rent abatements or organize anti-rent combinations during the 1885–6 period. None of the National League resolutions published in the *Kerry Sentinel* demanded a reduction in rent, but this needs to be seen in relation to the national leadership's stance towards agrarian agitation in the months preceding the defeat of Gladstone's home rule bill in June 1886. At this stage, Parnell was forced to distance himself and his party from purely agrarian agitation which had potentially violent consequences, so as to portray his movement as constitutional and law abiding in his quest for home rule. He declared in January 1886 that he and the Irish Parliamentary Party was doing all in their power to 'curb anti-rent combinations'.[18] In this context, it is not surprising that no resolutions demanding rent reductions were published in the *Kerry Sentinel*; however, this does not necessarily prove that no such activity occurred. For the month of April, DI Gray commented that 'the refusal to pay rent on Lord Ventry's property in this district is not the result of any inability to pay but the result of advice and examples [from the National League]'.[19] This statement demonstrates that the League was in some way involved in organizing rent strikes, yet it is difficult to determine the extent of such activity. From Gray's comments it would seem that the Dingle National League advised tenants to withhold rent rather than implemented a strict policy of prohibiting payment, as was the situation in other estates in the county. On the Kenmare estate, the National League courts regularly tried and punished those who paid without the demanded abatements.[20] As early as August 1885, Tim Healy, one of the leading National League figures in the country, advised tenants assembled at a meeting in Killarney to set up bank accounts to fund anti-rent combinations. Furthermore, this strategy was adopted on at least 12 estates in Co. Cork.[21] However, from the sources available it seems no such rigorous implementation of anti-rent combinations occurred in the Dingle region. Another area of landlord-tenant relations that the National League attempted to regulate was the purchasing of land by tenants under the terms of the 1885 Ashbourne Land Act. The National League condemned any transactions with the Land Commission and only gave approval to sales of land at a rate unacceptable to the landlord.[22] Prohibitions on land grabbing, purchasing of land and influence on the payment of rent were probably core of the League's policy in the Dingle area.

As the National League's campaign against landlordism intensified, the movement spread to much of the non-farming population. The very nature of boycotting necessitated the involvement of all sections of society, regardless of their interest in the landlord-tenant conflict. Furthermore, resolutions passed by particular branches deemed non-membership of the National League as an offence. One adopted proposal from the Camp branch illustrates this. It decided 'that no farmer in this parish employ a labourer or tradesman that is not a member of the National League or labourer work for any farmer who also is not a member of it'.[23] The National League had consolidated its support to a point where Gray stated that it 'is the only organization existing, it now embraces all except landlords'.[24] With this influx of new members into its ranks, the initial leadership axis of clergy–trader–strong farmer that prevailed during the emergence of the League remained intact: a meeting of the Dingle League in July was presided over by Fr Scully;[25] prominent farmers acted as vice-chairman and treasurer, and a publican in the town, Michael Murphy, sat as secretary.[26] Equally, the more rural Ballyferriter branch had a priest, Fr Kennedy, as its president[27] with a local shopkeeper in the position of treasurer and Maurice Ferriter (a prominent farmer) as chairman.[28]

While the National League maintained its traditional leadership, it counted on the support of many whose interests were not best served by the landlord-tenant conflict, particularly agricultural labourers, whose relationship with farmers was often acrimonious in the decades after the Famine, as Irish farmers turned away from labour intensive tillage. The number of agricultural labourers decreased from over half the population in 1841 to less than a third in 1911.[29] By the 1880s, this class had a long list of grievances with farmers over housing, machinery, conacre rents and wages and generally regarded them as cunning adversaries and class enemies.[30] During the 1870s, labourers became increasingly politicized and agitated through the extension of the British National Agricultural Union to Ireland. However, by 1879 the union was dwarfed by the emerging Land League and ceased to exist in Ireland.[31] Historians' views differ on the role of labourers and the support they gave to the 1879–82 agitation. Many maintain that labourers were too weak to agitate effectively and had no option but to support the League.[32] Samuel Clark has argued that League organizers were indifferent to labourers – a fact that reflected not only their unimportance but also their alienation from the movement.[33] On the other hand, Paul Bew suggests that the Land League seriously tried to promote labourers' interests out of fear that they might otherwise alienate a powerful group.[34]

By 1885, the support of agricultural labourers was clearly sought by the National League. In his speech that led to the establishment of the League in Dingle, Harrington applauded the class by 'paying a tribute of respect to the earnest patriotic and unselfish service which the agricultural labourers have given to the farmers of this country in this movement'.[35] The League's courting of agricultural labourers indicates that they were viewed as an important interest group in the rural community. This importance was undoubtedly increased after the enfranchisement of some 400,000 in the Reform Act of 1884, which gave many small tenants and labourers voting power for the first time.[36] As the National League called for labourer support for a movement that would largely benefit their class adversaries, the unionist press sensed an opportunity to gain backing for unionist candidates in the county in the general election of 1885. In the run-up to the general election, articles appeared in the *Kerry Evening Post*, the unionist newspaper in Kerry, aimed at increasing tensions between labourers and farmers by arguing that labourer grievances were not with landlords but with farmers.[37] Hence, the attempted lobbying of agricultural labourers by both nationalists and unionists suggested that they were of some political importance in mid-1880s Irish society.

However, landlords had neither the organizational ability nor the power to compete with the National League in attracting agricultural labourer support for unionism, and in reality the threat of boycotting was strong enough to ensure that labourers would remain within the realms of the League. In the National League itself, there is evidence to suggest that they were active, for we find pro-labourer resolutions being formulated in the branches. A branch in Ballylongford in northern Kerry deemed that 'any man holding not less than 20 acres and refusing to give a plot of one acre to the labourer be immediately expelled'.[38] In the Dingle area, labourers on the whole remained outside the leadership, but one did reach the committee in the Camp branch.[39] That branch actively pioneered labourer causes. On one occasion a labourer complained that a farming member of the League did not supply him with a conacre plot at a reduced rate set by the League:[40] the branch passed a resolution demanding that the farmer make good the labourer's losses.[41] Another resolution from the Dingle branch proposed that 'all labourers in this locality [be] supplied near the sea shore with conacre plots at half the customary rates'.[42] In many cases, the National League championed labourers' demands, particularly in relation to conacre rents, to the detriment of farmers. (Despite this, labourers made little impact on the overall leadership, as farmers' objectives of lowering rents and preventing evictions remained the dominant factors behind National League activity.) While these examples of labourer action within the movement demonstrate the importance of the class during this period, they also portray a widening of the National League's agenda. Social issues that were not directly related to the landlord-tenant conflict were coming under its jurisdiction. Through its 'court' system, it began regulating many aspects of rural life in Dingle. One example of this was the case of the carriers in Dingle. The carriers, whose livelihood depended on transporting goods, complained that they were 'idle on account of all the farmers sending their horses into town to do all their cartage'. The League responded proclaiming that the farmers of the region had to use the carriers' service.[43] The extension of National League involvement into matters such as this illustrates that, as it consolidated its membership across the social spectrum, it came to represent the needs of all of its members. Furthermore, it was a reflection of the League's power and authority as it was forcing its own economic and social policies upon society at large.

As the authority of the National League increased, the power of landlordism was undermined. Rent collection became problematic as evictions became increasingly difficult to enforce and landlords were on the receiving end of rigorous boycotting. The 'League courts', whose primary purpose it was to force landlords to yield to tenants' demands, dominated most of society. Such was the situation during the poor law elections in March 1886 to elect candidates for the boards of guardians. Since the initiation of the land war there was an attempt by various League branches at local level throughout the country to oust the landlord gentry from the controlling positions of the poor law. The issue of tackling landlord control on the boards of guardians received little support from the Irish Parliamentary Party and the national leadership. In Harrington's original speech at Dingle in May 1885 his only reference to the issue was a vague demand for local government reform placed firmly behind home rule and land reform in his list of priorities.[44] However, local branches of both the Land and National Leagues were very interested in the poor law elections as they became a vehicle to challenge landlords and acquire a degree of power on a local level. By 1886, according to William Feingold, 244 of the controlling positions of all the boards of guardians in the country were in the hands of the tenantry compared to only 59 in 1877.[45] This transformation of power was co-ordinated by local League branches who selected nationalist candidates, formulated strategies and organized voters at election time. Such League involvement was evident in the run-up to the 1886 poor law election in Dingle where the board of guardians was traditionally dominated by the local gentry. Lord Ventry was chairman while his nephew Edward de Moleyns acted as vice-chairman and another member of the gentry, A.E. Hickson, was deputy vice-chairman.[46] A convention of delegates from the various local League branches was held[47] for the purpose of contesting the election and anyone who campaigned against the National League candidate was boycotted. Uncharacteristically, the local press virtually ignored the run up to the contest and gave no coverage to the event. Notwithstanding this, out of the 22 seats those nominated by the National League won 20.[48] During the first meeting of the new board, the National League candidates easily defeated the unionist challenge, with John Lee, a founding member of the League in the town and a hotel owner, being appointed chairman. Other leading League members elected to the board included Michael O'Donnell and Thomas Kelliher, both prominent farmers. The nationalist sentiments of the new board were illustrated in its initial resolutions that expressed support for Home Rule along with the promise to tackle the plight of the poor.[49]

As a result of this *de facto* transfer of power in Dingle's local government, the National League had potentially an extremely powerful weapon in its control. Through the patronage of contracts and relief work, the League could further enhance its position within society while continuing to use its traditional methods of obstructing evictions and boycotting. In turn, the unionist press claimed that League-dominated boards suffered from misadministration and massive over-spending on relief works. In one damning report, to a select committee of the house of lords examining the Poor Law Guardian bill in 1884, an inspector gave evidence claiming that when boards came under League control relief expenditure rose and was granted on political grounds to help evicted tenants.[50] However, the situation was more complicated, and the use of large amounts of poor relief for political ends had its drawbacks for the boards. An increase in relief was reflected in a rise in the poor law rate set by the board. Although the landlord of the holding paid anything from three-fifths to three-quarters of this tax, any increases were bitterly opposed by tenants.[51] Also, by the time the League in Dingle acquired control on the board, an increase in taxation seemed unlikely because of the difficulty in collecting existing arrears. Financially, the Dingle union was in a chronic state and close to bankruptcy. On the eve of the National League election success, the board was informed 'that the bank manager declines to have anything to do with Guardian cheques until account is put in a more business like manner'.[52] Due to the unstable political situation and the agricultural depression, the rate-collectors were unable to extract poor law rates. By June 1886, of the total owed from the previous April, only half were paid.[53] Hence, the ability of the League to extend its influence through granting relief was seriously undermined. Despite the League's original commitment to help the poor, people seeking relief were frequently turned away empty-handed.[54]

As the League-dominated board attempted to establish its influence in the Dingle union it was often met with resistance by its controlling body, the Local Government Board for Ireland. Acting as a control centre for the poor law unions, this board was answerable to the chief secretary's office. It employed an effective and efficient body of inspectors that rigorously supervised the activity of the poor law unions, ensuring that they remained within the law and acted in accordance with the rules and regulations governing the boards.[55] During the period between 1880 and 1890, as many as 13 individual unions were dissolved by the Local Government Board.[56] While many of these dissolutions were effected for failure by the boards to carry out their duties correctly, the Local Government Board seem to have actively targeted nationalist-controlled unions. This was the case when the local government inspector for the Dingle union, Colonel Spaight (an active unionist),[57] began opposing the nationalist members of the board. After the successful National League-inspired victory in the poor law election, the guardians were forced to re-nominate the officers to the chairs of the board as their original nomination was deemed invalid by the Local Government Board.[58] Although this was only a formality and the original new nominees were reinstated, the policy of obstructionism towards the new board continued. In an attempt to redress the ailing finances of the board, the guardians recommended that 'salaries of all officers connected with the union including the cost of dispensary will be reduced to a standard proportional to the depression of the times'[59] but this was rebuked by the Local Government Board. The two authorities clashed again when the guardians elected Patrick Ferriter, the secretary of the Ballyferriter National League, as the relieving officer for the Dingle and Ventry districts.[60] Obviously politically motivated, the Local Government Board reacted by claiming that due to physical deficiency Ferriter was not capable of carrying out the intended tasks.[61] In reply, the guardians sent a medical report declaring Ferriter fit for the job. Despite this, the Local Government Board refused to accept him and by the following month his appointment had to be relinquished.[62] After the nationalist attainment of power on the board of guardians, the unionist ex-officio members refused to sit on it, yet the activities of the remaining National League-backed members were seriously undermined. The chronic financial predicament of the union meant that the League could not gain political advantage through the granting of relief. Similarly, the overriding power of the Local Government Board handicapped much of the board's business; this extended from refusing government grants to interfering with the board's legitimate selection of employees. However, the defeat of Lord Ventry by the National League forces symbolized the declining influence of landlordism and the increased influence of the League.

3. The decline and fall of the League

By mid-1886 the Dingle National League was in an unassailable position. It was successfully tackling the dominance of landlordism as the 'League courts' were gaining authority over the local population. The National League were not just regulating landlord-tenant relations but also influencing other sections of the community (agricultural labourers, for example). Furthermore, the National League utilized its extensive structural organization to gain control of local government by removing Lord Ventry from the chairmanship of the board of guardians and in the process denied the landlord class of the area a traditional source of power. At the heart of this dramatic rise in power and stature was its prime weapon, the boycott. However, this method of agitation was to create untold pressure within the National League in the Dingle area through exhaustive and abusive enactment of the policy.

As Parnell and his lieutenants fought principally for home rule, the national leadership forcibly discouraged boycotting, as they attempted to maintain the National League's legitimacy. The secretary of the central branch, Timothy Harrington, when writing to a Fr Gilchrist in an area in Co. Cork, outlined his attitude towards boycotting. He urged the priest 'in the direction of condemning the practice', while Parnell publicly announced that the National League 'were doing everything in their power to stamp out boycotting'.[1] The situation on the ground in Dingle, however, could not have been more different. In the same month as Parnell's statement, it was reported that 'Dingle is perhaps the most active centre of boycotting at present in this country'.[2] Within a couple of months, boycotting was reaching such unprecedented levels in the region that it was coming to the attention of the central branch. Writing to the Ballyferriter League after receiving a complaint from a man who claimed he was been unjustly boycotted, Timothy Harrington warned, 'I hope your branch will not allow itself to be led into an extreme or unreasonable course of action.'[3] By this stage the League had been in existence for just over a year and cracks were beginning to emerge in its strength and unity. The Ballyferriter branch complained at a National League meeting that 'the Dingle tradesmen and shopkeepers are dealing with boycotted parties of this district indiscriminately'.[4] In response to this accusation, the secretary of the Dingle League, M.W. Murphy (a publican from Green Street in Dingle town), condemned the Ballyferriter branch for adopting 'a wholesale system of boycotting'.[5] The dissension that arose between the two branches emerged after the Dingle League refused to extend its boycott to a list of names issued by the Ballyferriter branch. In a letter to central branch, Murphy maintained 'that they [Ballyferriter] are wrong in supplying us [Dingle] a list of fourteen obnoxious persons in one slap',[6] while claiming that 'the Ballyferriter branch are acting in the most ridiculous manner, in a way which I believe will cause incalculable injury to the movement'.[7] Influenced by what Murphy said, Harrington warned the Ballyferriter branch 'that they ought to do nothing that would endanger the National cause'.[8] The turmoil carried on when members of the Ballyferriter branch attended a Dingle League meeting to air their differences. They alleged that Murphy 'had neglected his duty by not having got the Dingle branch to adopt a series of resolutions furnished to him' after which they were 'scouted out of the room'.[9] This whole episode illustrated the increasing internal pressure building up inside the League. However, it is difficult to determine the precise cause of this tension, which led to social conflict between two branches. One possible suggestion is that there was a social conflict between the rural Ballyferriter branch and the more urban Dingle League, although the leadership of both branches comprised of large farmers and traders. Whatever the source of dissension, it was apparent that cracks were beginning to emerge in the unity of the National League.

Developments within the Dingle branch itself led to increased division in the movement. Signs of strife among members of the Dingle National League had initially emerged by July when Murphy complained that boycotting was being overused for what he described as 'for any or every cause'.[10] This division was worsened by the commencement of the boycott on the Clyde Shipping Company by the Dingle League, on the complaint 'that she's bringing to every obnoxious [boycotted] person in the district'.[11] While the company that sailed from Cork to Dingle was shipping goods to boycotted persons, such as William Collier, the service was also an integral part of the town's commercial heart. Under *Slater's directory* description of Dingle in 1881 the company was described as being 'of great advantage to its [Dingle's] traders'.[12] Complaints were lodged at central branch over the issue, this resulted in Harrington writing a scalding letter to the Dingle League, in which he observed 'It is strange that your [Dingle] branch is the only one in the south of Ireland from which at present we receive numerous complaints of this kind of boycotting.'[13] Aware of the potential danger, he warned that 'it would be very foolish to force the local traders to give up dealing with the Steam Ship Company'.[14] Within a month, Murphy claimed that 'the members themselves seemed divided over the business' and that the boycott was harming the town commercially.[15] With little alternative available to Harrington due to constant complaints emerging from the region over the abuse of boycotting and the divided nature of the Dingle National League, he dissolved the branch.[16] As with the Ballyferriter situation, it is hard to establish what lay at the heart of the conflict within the Dingle League. Some evidence suggests that it was class-based and between farmers and shopkeepers. In a later letter to the Dingle region, Timothy Harrington expressed the view that the boycott on the Clyde Shipping Company was 'a policy calculated to do injury to the shopkeeping community in Dingle'.[17] If this was the case, it demonstrates that the alliance between shopkeepers and farmers that formed much of the leadership of the National League not only in Dingle but also across the country was not as unified and coherent as many contemporary commentators thought. However, political divisions may also have had a part to play in the conflict. From the language that the secretary, Murphy, used, it may be inferred that he was a Home Ruler and a constitutional nationalist. He claimed he only joined 'for the national cause'. Furthermore, much of his rhetoric may be seen as moderate. At one stage he complained that the Dingle League was 'ruled by force rather than reason',[18] while on another occasion he criticized some members of the Dingle and Ballyferriter branches for acting in a ridiculous manner for rigorously enforcing boycotts,[19] suggesting there were more extreme forces dictating League policy. Whether the conflict was based on class or political divisions, tensions were definitely high within the Dingle and Ballyferriter National League branches proving that the movement locally was racked by rifts and the competing needs of its membership.

The closure of the Dingle branch of the National League led to a weakening of the organization in the region, causing the unionist press to joyously proclaim that the League was losing its hold over the people (the *Kerry Sentinel* completely ignored the dissolution).[20] However, the event did not signal the end of the League, as Harrington was made aware of the urgent need for a active branch in Dingle.[21] By October, he had granted permission for the reorganization of the Dingle League on the condition that the local priest Fr Scully, supervised the affair and the boycott of the Clyde Shipping Boat should not continue.[22] Within a couple of months, the Dingle National League once again came to the attention of Harrington. The issue this time centred on the boycotting of a Mrs Benner who after acquiring a hotel in the town found herself the subject of League harassment. Harrington, who knew the lady, remarked that she was a 'strong nationalist' and warned the Dingle League that if the boycott was not stopped,

> I shall certainly again dissolve the branch and if I am driven to do so again as long as I have anything to do in the National League they will have no branch in Dingle. We [central branch] regard the conduct of the Dingle branch of the National League was grossly unpatriotic.[23]

The reasons behind Harrington's condemnatory language become clearer when the motives for the boycott are examined. It was claimed that the boycott was initiated to please Mr Lee, chairman of the board of guardians and founding member of the League.[24] Considering Lee's occupation as a hotel owner, the reasons for the boycott become more apparent as the establishment of another hotel in the town may have harmed his business. In this instance, the pursuit of personal gain by some of its members is revealed as another motive behind much National League activity. Presumably other boycotts were part of personal vendettas – which may indicate the reason for the constant complaints coming from the area.

During the turmoil within the National League movement in the Dingle region, the political situation was changing nationally as the agricultural depression and the failure of Gladstone's home rule bill forced the leadership to refocus. Inevitably, it was the land question which re-emerged as the principal focus of agitation after the parliamentary effort of attaining home rule was dealt a blow when the Conservatives gained control of the house of commons in 1886. The new agitation was defined by the establishment of what became known as the 'Plan of Campaign', in the late autumn of 1886. Originally drawn up by Timothy Harrington, the 'Plan' involved the declaration of rent strikes on estates where landlords refused to grant abatements of rent. Tenants paid what they considered to be a fair rent into a common fund that was to be used to further the campaign and to support evicted tenants.[25] Enacted on 203 estates in the country,[26] the resulting battles were subject to intense coverage in the press as they had an implicit political role and came to be seen as a trial of strength between the National League (backed by the tenants) and the landlords with government support.

To bolster support for the 'Plan', national figures embarked on a series of speeches throughout the country. In similar circumstances to the emergence of the National League in Dingle, Edward Harrington addressed a public meeting at Dingle in early January 1887 for the purpose of extending the new national policy, although this time he was accompanied by an English MP named Conbeare.[27] The event was an exercise in nationalist propaganda as

> about 300 horsemen bedecked with green sashes and ribbons met these gentlemen some miles from Dingle and escorted them into town with band playing and banners flying, about 3000 people attended the meeting.[28]

This form of mass meeting in itself was part of the technique of the campaign, as it gave tenants a sense of their collective strength and impressed landlords with the wisdom of accepting a reasonable offer rather than face a long and costly struggle.[29] Although it was advertised as a National League meeting, all the local speakers were members of the clergy (indicative of the clerical support the new agitation attracted). The speakers in the main dealt with the land question and encouraged the 'Plan of Campaign' while also condemning the recent imprisonment of the leading national advocates of the 'Plan', William O'Brien and John Dillon. Interestingly, home rule was not mentioned: this reflected the shift in policy towards agrarian issues by sections of the national leadership. The strongest indication that the 'Plan' was to be adopted in the Dingle area emerged after one of the local priests claimed that he had received rents from an estate where the landlord refused to grant a 30 per cent abatement in rent to the tenants, a central element of the Plan.[30] Where implemented, the 'Plan' often led to protracted, violent and dogged conflicts between the tenantry and the landlord. However, it ended relatively quickly on the Dingle Peninsula in one episode that became known as the 'Ballyferriter Evictions'.

The new national strategy formulated by the Plan of Campaign was extended to the Dingle region by a public meeting in early 1887 which led to a 'universal strike against rent' on a section of Lord Cork's estate in Ballyferriter.[31] Shortly after this, 11 eviction notices were served to tenants on the estate. Evictions in the area were at times met with resistance (usually taking the form of hostile crowds gathering to jeer the eviction party, as bailiffs, aided by police forced their way into barricaded homes), but for the most part they passed off without any major incident. Yet, in the light of the renewed agitation, the tenantry was in a defiant mood as extensive measures were put in place to stop the evictions. The main road between Dingle and Ballyferriter was cut, and stone walls were built as obstructions, forcing the eviction party to take another route.[32] On arrival in Ballyferriter, a large, menacing, crowd of '3–4,000 with bludgeons, pikes, scythes and sharp edged-shovels'[33] that had assembled to resist the evictions met the police and bailiffs. A tense stand-off ensued where the police were ordered 'to fix bayonets and load with buckshot' which led to a man in the crowd shouting 'Stand by your pikes, men' to the crowd.[34] Violence and bloodshed were avoided as the police withdrew without implementing any of the evictions.

Despite the initial unsuccessful attempt at the evictions, defeat was not on the mind of the constabulary. With the Plan of Campaign gathering momentum nationally, a League victory in resisting the Ballyferriter evictions would have provided the movement with much propaganda and would have seriously undermined the police, landlords and government policy in general. It became a matter of urgent importance for the under-secretary of the time, General Redvers Buller. Buller had come to Ireland the previous September and was appointed divisional magistrate for Kerry and Clare with orders from the new Conservative government to curb agitation by reorganising the police force.[35] Although he became known for holding sympathetic views towards the tenants at the expense of landlords (albeit combined with contempt for the National League),[36] he was determined to enforce the evictions in Ballyferriter. Under the command of a former district inspector for Dingle, Charles Crane, he sent a force of over 100 policemen to Dingle. In

5 Poster advertising a National League meeting in Dingle where speakers called for the 'Plan of Campaign' to be implemented in the region.
Source: NAI, ISO, RP BOX 3310/1887.

Crane's memoirs he recalls how after leaving for Dingle the murder of a land agent was committed in his current district. After telegraphing Buller as to whether he ought to return to deal with the serious crime, his orders were to carry on to Dingle owing to the importance of the task.[37] After he arrived in Dingle he recalled the effects of boycotting where his tired and hungry men had great difficulty in finding food and accommodation.[38] Indeed, the National League was extremely active as it enforced boycotts on the police and eviction party. To maximize the extent of the boycott, shops were closed and business totally suspended, 'circulars were passed to bakers not to bake bread and butchers not to cut meat'.[39] In effect, the town shut down against the arriving police force. In return, proclamations were issued in the town warning that attempts to stop the evictions would be met with force. The eviction expedition recommenced it duties on 25 February with a police force of 140.[40] Scenes similar to the previous effort at the evictions ensued as obstacles were put in the way of the eviction party and an effort was made to demolish a bridge en route to Ballyferriter.[41] Once again, on entering Ballyferriter they were met by tenants lining the hilltops along the road. This time, however, the land agent met with the local clergy and a settlement was made leading to a potentially violent situation passing off peacefully with an abatement being made in the rent.[42]

The whole episode illustrated that, despite the League's internal difficulties in the Dingle area, it remained an influential organization in the local community. Its considerable local power was once again demonstrated, as it enforced boycotts and organized the tenants to withstand the authorities, leading to a reduction in rent. However, repercussions were to be felt by the League where criminal charges were brought against 26 men for their part in resisting the evictions. The majority were not prosecuted as the judge deemed that they were 'led astray', but Michael Dissette and Patrick Foley (both founding members of the League) and a man named O'Donoghue were each jailed for three months on refusal to pay their fines.[43]

After the 'Ballyferriter evictions', the Plan of Campaign was not readopted on any of the properties in the Dingle region. Very little enthusiasm was shown for it in Kerry as a whole, as it was fought out on only five estates, the second lowest number of any county in Munster.[44] Notwithstanding this, the National League continued in its enthusiasm in enforcing boycotts. For the month of March 1887 the county inspector commented: 'there is a good deal of boycotting about Dingle, the National League is pretty much the same.'[45] Despite this, the National League was to face stiff opposition from the authorities. Arthur Balfour, the chief secretary, who had replaced the largely ineffectual Hicks-Beach, was proving far more competent. He set about introducing a new Crimes bill to counter the National League and the Plan of Campaign.[46] By April 1887, the south-western division of the RIC (comprising some of the most disturbed places in Kerry, Clare and parts of

Cork) was declared as generally 'improved, fear of coming crimes bill has had a great effect', while the county inspector for Kerry claimed that the 'League seems languishing everywhere'.[47] During June, the Dingle branch members were failing to renew subscriptions,[48] an indication of the League's waning support and influence. Lord Ventry carried out a number of evictions on his property unhindered and with none of the scenes that accompanied the Ballyferriter evictions the pervious February.[49] Speaking of Kerry as a whole for July, the county inspector commented 'that the state of the county is fairly satisfactory, rents and debts been collected without bailiffs ... the National League is weak in Kerry, Dingle branch is the most active but dread of Crimes Act keeps them fairly quiet'.[50] On Lord Cork's property, rents were being collected at a satisfactory rate, and it was reported that 'the relations between the landlord and tenants have never been of a more friendly nature'.[51] The position of the National League was definitely beginning to sway in Dingle from its previous dominant stature and the introduction of the new legislation was to have catastrophic results for the future of the League.

The Criminal Law and Procedure (Ireland) Act introduced by the Chief Secretary Balfour in the autumn of 1887 was an extremely powerful piece of legislation. It gave the RIC and the judiciary (largely through the resident magistrates who sat at the petty session) the necessary powers to combat the National League. The summary jurisdiction powers of the 1882 Crimes Act were revived; this enabled the authorities to successfully curb anti-rent combinations, boycotting and intimidation. Other important powers were added to the new Crimes Act. Section 7 gave the lord lieutenant the authority to announce specific regions 'proclaimed' and to identify individual branches of the National League as dangerous associations and therefore illegal.[52] Furthermore, the police were empowered to disperse meetings of suppressed branches, arrest ringleaders, and stop publication of League material in the press.[53] Utilizing the new legislation, the barony of Corkaguiny in which Dingle was the principal town was proclaimed on 17 September 1887.[54] Notices were posted on the walls and courthouses outlawing and suppressing the National League in the region.[55] The whole country was not proclaimed – only certain districts and branches where the agitation and League activity was extensive. Along with parts of Clare and Kerry, baronies in Donegal, Mayo, Queen's County, Roscommon, Tipperary and Waterford were proclaimed with a further 50 branches suppressed in the space of 26 months. In all, the government suppressed 185 out of the League's 1,130 branches.[56]

The district inspector for Dingle, Alexander Gray, took great satisfaction in the criminialization of an organization that had undermined the constabulary's authority; he triumphantly remarked, 'the corner boys are sullen, their reign is nearly at an end'.[57] The new legislation had an immediate effect. By November 1887 the county inspector for Kerry commented that the 'change in Dingle is most remarkable' and believed that that 'the people (are) beginning to see the law is too strong'.[58] Gray was of the same opinion on the demise of the League, as he described how Kearney, a land agent for Lord Cork, 'couldn't buy tobacco twelve months ago but now no problem and that those who have been boycotted for a long time are now able to purchase goods without any trouble openly'.[59] In the same report he expressed his confidence in the beneficial effects of the Crimes Act in counteracting the League, commenting that 'continued and uncompromising firmness in administering the law is all that is needed to restore peace'. Another government official echoed his sentiments when he stated, 'it remains to be shown whether the body of leaguers are prepared to undergo imprisonment by open violation of the law. No doubt a few wild spirits will but the mass of the Irish farmer will not adopt it.'[60]

However, resistance was forthcoming from the National League activists. In breach of the coercion laws, the *Kerry Sentinel* continued to publish reports from branches in suppressed areas, including Dingle. Resolutions from these National League reports indicated their intentions. The Dingle branch declared: 'we shall continue to uphold our meetings and defy them and all the rent office gang'.[61] In turn, the police vigorously attempted to break up League meetings; this often led to violence. Police action was consolidated by strict enforcement of the law by the resident magistrates sitting on the bench of the crimes courts. In January 1888, Cecil Roche, a magistrate who became notorious for his rigid implementation of the Crimes Act,[62] warned that he would 'come out myself and teach those Ballyferriter people to be quiet'[63] after violent incidents occurred between police and National League supporters during an illegal meeting. During the same hearing, Roche imposed prison sentences for illegal assembly on four people who had obstructed the police at a National League meeting.[64] At another crimes court hearing, Roche again applied the law in a severe manner, when, in relation to disturbances between National League supporters and the police, he warned that 'this scandalous conduct must be put down and it will be put down'.[65]

Such stringent implementation of the law was vigorously carried through as the authorities targeted the leaders of the National League. In an attempt to renew their spirit licences, Michael Dissette, John Lee (chairman of the board of guardians) and W.M. McCarthy (former secretary of the League) appeared before the courts in late 1887. All were leading and founding members of the National League in the Dingle region. Their applications were denied on the grounds that they neglected to carry out their legal duties by refusing to serve policemen during the 'Ballyferriter evictions'.[66] Dissette was condemned because the prosecution asserted 'that for the last twelve months [he] acted in the strongest antipathy to the police and he therefore did not think he was a fit and proper person to have a publican's license'.[67] All three were refused renewals of their spirit licences, and therefore a major source of income, because of their National League activity. Furthermore, League leaders received prison sentences. Timothy Harrington, the secretary of the Central branch of the National League, was arrested and imprisoned for six weeks for the publication of reports from branches in proclaimed districts in the *Kerry Sentinel*.[68] In the Dingle region, Patrick Ferriter, former secretary of both the Ballyferriter and Dingle National Leagues, became the subject of much police attention. He was the first person to be imprisoned under the new Crimes Act in the area. Initially he was sentenced to two weeks' hard labour for assaulting a policeman.[69] Despite this, Ferriter had become one of the leading League figures after its suppression. He was before Cecil Roche RM again in April 1888 for selling a copy of *United Ireland* (the nation-wide League newspaper) containing a report of a meeting from a suppressed branch in Co. Clare. On refusing a request not to continue selling the paper, Roche sentenced him to three months' hard labour.[70] The sentence was deemed extremely harsh because the case was brought long after the government had stopped the policy of prosecuting newspaper vendors.[71] The *Kerry Sentinel* denounced Roche's actions in its editorial, while nationalist MPs raised the issue in the house of commons. W.A. Donald MP wondered if there was 'any true freedom of press in Ireland', and John Redmond called for his immediate release.[72]

As the police, led by D.I. Gray and fully supported by the judiciary, vigorously implemented the coercion laws, the National League was seriously undermined and the agrarian agitation declined. By January 1888, less than four months after the introduction of the Crimes Act, it was reported to the chief secretary's office that ' the Criminal Law and Procedure (Ire.) Act has in the suppression of disorder and resistance to the law been uniformly successful in its operation'.[73] By April 1888, while giving evidence against Ferriter, Gray declared in reference to the Dingle area that 'there is a very marked improvement since the beginning of the year, everything is very quite at present' and more significantly 'boycotting has ceased'.[74] He may well have been exaggerating, but boycotting levels had indeed declined: see table 3.

Table 3. Number of boycotting cases reported to the RIC in Co. Kerry between October 1887 and March 1889

1887	1888				1889
Oct.–Dec.	Jan.–Mar.	Apr.–June	July–Sept.	Oct.–Dec.	Jan.–Mar.
1037	388	240	179	158	93

Source: CSO, Crime Branch Special: Divisional Commissioners' and County Inspectors' monthly confidential reports, carton 4 (National Archives)

Furthermore, while giving evidence Gray claimed that there were no National League meetings taking place and that those reported in the press were 'bogus';[75] they were merely concocted and by one of its members; RIC sources were of the opinion that 'branches [are] not progressing in activity, several meetings are published and resolutions shown [and] passed on to the newspapers which never happened'.[76] Out of 27 meetings of suppressed branches in Kerry reported during February and March 1888, 22 were considered 'bogus'.[77] The reports that appeared in the *Kerry Sentinel* for the Dingle region had the hallmarks of being such 'bogus' meetings. They no longer resembled the previous 'League courts' where witnesses, evidence and pleas dominated the reports. Resolutions passed dealt with broad issues such as the condemnation of high profile arrests or offering support for the 'Plan of Campaign'; moreover, names of committee members rarely appeared in full. The characteristic features of League reports were absent, indicating that these reports were in fact 'bogus'. By April 1888, the offensive against the National League was seriously weakening the organization. The force of the law had successfully disrupted its meetings and imprisoned its leaders, and publicans who were leading members of the League had their licenses revoked. The League's 'court system' became unworkable as the police constantly curtailed meetings. Without the infrastructure of its weekly meetings, the League's highly effective, and its sophisticated system of boycotting was undermined until it verged on extinction. The 'League courts' and boycotting were the key to League power and authority. As these fundamental aspects of League control were undermined, so was the League itself.

The impact of the legislation implemented by the Conservative government aimed at solving the Irish land question also precipitated the decrease of the National League agitation. The National League forcibly discouraged the Ashbourne Act 1885 as it deemed it did not favour tenants. However, Chief Secretary Balfour's land reform measures, which began with the Land Act of August 1887, offered better conditions for tenants and decreased the likelihood of eviction, thereby reducing the discontent that might spark further agrarian agitation.[78] While it is difficult to establish the extent to which this act was implemented in the Dingle region (no estate papers are available), it did have a calming effect on much of the country. The little evidence available concerning abatements in rent given by the landlords in the area suggests that reductions were made. In January 1889, it was reported in the *Kerry Evening Post* that Lord Cork's tenantry 'paid their rents, less twenty per cent' and that 'LordVentry's agent has being receiving rent giving the usual allowances of twenty-five per cent'.[79]

With the winding down of National League activity, due to the vigorous implementation of the Crimes Act coupled with increasingly favourably terms for the tenantry, the next centre of League power targeted by the authorities was inevitably the board of guardians. The poor law elections of March 1888 became another battleground between the National League and the increasingly powerful forces of the state and landlordism. Deprived of the fully effective branch system that underpinned National League electoral dominance in the past (at both local and national level), its ability to successfully contest the election was severely limited. However, it was active in Dingle, as it was reported that 'members of the suppressed Irish National League called at the houses of nearly all the ratepayers with a view of intimidating them from voting for one of the candidates [James Farrell] and against their nominee [John Lee]'.[80] Significantly, this League activity failed to prevent it from incurring serious losses at the election. The headline of the Conservative *Kerry Evening Post* joyously proclaimed 'the League worsened' as numerous nationalist candidates lost their seats.[81] Undoubtedly, the most high-profile League defeat was that of John Lee, the outgoing National League chairman of the Dingle board of guardians. Despite the League's failings, it narrowly managed to maintain control of the board. The new candidates elected Maurice O'Connor over Lord Ventry as chairman by the tightest of margins of ten votes to nine.[82] While the League succeeded in controlling the board, the losses inflicted on it were representative of its waning support and authority. At its height, the League ensured up to twenty guardians supported its candidate for chairman.[83] However, this figure was halved after the 1888 election. The new anti-National League guardians were representative of the class of prominent farmer that had provided much of the League leadership in the past (Nicholas Fitzgerald elected to the electoral division of Cloghane after defeating the outgoing National League guardian was listed in *Guy's directory* as a prominent farmer).[84] Furthermore, it soon became apparent that existing guardians who had sat on the National League-dominated boards had switched allegiances and voted for Lord Ventry against the League; an example of this was John Long, another prominent farmer elected to the Dunurlin division.[85] Even more interesting was the case of Timothy Flaherty, a founding member of the National League in Dingle (he appeared on the platform of the original meeting in May 1885).[86] Throughout the agitation he remained active in the Dingle League, at times corresponding with Timothy Harrington on behalf of the branch.[87] As late as June 1887, three months before the suppression of the National League, he was listed as attending a Dingle branch meeting in the *Kerry Sentinel*.[88] However, by the time of the 1888 poor law union elections he was actively opposed to the League. He was elected to the Dingle division, defeating John Lee and Thomas Kelliher, both co-founders of the Dingle branch and Flaherty's former League colleagues. He supported Lord Ventry in his quest for the chairmanship of the board and ran for the position of vice-chairman, only to be defeated by the League nominee, Daniel O'Connell.

The defeat of National League candidates during the elections and the emergence of anti-League guardians who had previously actively supported the movement before its suppression, depicted the waning strength and popularity of the League. Yet, it is difficult to determine the motives behind these new anti-League guardians. Economically, many were the same class of prominent farmer as the National League guardians. Politically, Flaherty and Michael Hanifin (he defeated the National League guardian for Kinard) maintained they were nationalists, and indicated this in their proposal for the board to adopt a resolution that condemned the imprisonment of 'William O'Brien by his political opponent, 'the brutal Balfour'.[89] Despite such class and political similarities, these guardians had become profoundly opposed to the National League in the Dingle region. While this complex situation suggests a schism in the League locally, there is little evidence to determine what lay at the heart of it. The RIC were of the opinion that many in society were exasperated with the agitation. The county inspector for Kerry voiced the belief that, 'I think the older men and respectable farmers and shopkeepers are tired of the state of things which has existed and would be glad of an administration of the law of the officials.'[90] Furthermore, Gray, the district inspector for Dingle, considered that the 'more respectable people [were] long sick of it [National League] but owing to the reign of terror that prevailed were afraid to sever their connection'.[91] Although such comments may have been designed to justify official policy, the emergence of anti-National League voters and guardians indicates that they had some basis in reality. With the power the League achieved through the boycott undermined, sections within society formerly coerced into supporting the movement now had the ability to dissent. However, other reasons may explain the rise of a strong anti-National League vote. In the 1889 poor law election the *Kerry Sentinel* claimed that for 'some days prior to the elections Lord Ventry's bailiffs ... [were] seen openly coercing the tenants and threatening anyone who dared to support a national candidate' and that League losses were a result of 'landlord terrorism'.[92] While the collapse in National League power potentially strengthened the landlord class, their position must not be overstated. The traditional power that landlords derived from the threat to evict had been largely removed after the 1887 Land Act, and their overall position at the end of the decade was one of an ailing class with little future. Other motives behind the actions of the anti-League guardians may have been the pursuit of individual power and influence on the board. If the National League had been ousted from the controlling positions of the board, Timothy Flaherty was to be elected vice-chairman, a position previously preserved for Lord Ventry's brother and land agent, Edward de Molyean. Whatever the determining factors behind the rise of anti-National League guardians in Dingle, it was clear that a sizeable minority within sections of society that previously supported the League were politically agitating against the organization by the time of the 1888 poor law election.

After the failed attempt to return the board of guardians to the control of Lord Ventry, District Inspector Gray initiated a campaign against the National League guardians. He reported in April 1888 to the chief secretary's office that the board was merely a tool of National League power. Central to this claim was the role of Patrick Ferriter. By mid 1888 Ferriter had become the leading National League figure in Dingle. The harsh treatment bestowed on him by the authorities had gained him a certain degree of martyrdom both locally and nationally. The *Kerry Sentinel* used his case as a propaganda tool to highlight the injustices of the Crimes Act and the government in general. The RIC sergeant at Dingle, Moran, wrote of Ferriter's influence on the board: '[he] attends each meeting of the board ... whatever he purposes or puts forward is sure to pass unanimously'.[93] Moran maintained that Ferriter's power was based on League activity and that guardians were 'afraid he would write to all the other suppressed branches of the League in the district for the purpose of having them held up as traitors to the national cause'.[94] Gray echoed his sergeant's sentiments by stating that 'Ferriter is allowed to attend the board as a reporter but in reality he is there as the representative of the National League and is consulted on by the Guardians on everything', adding, Ferriter 'is constantly in prison and he is a regular gaol bird'.[95] The credibility of Gray's assertions have to be questioned, considering the ailing position of the League at this period and the emergence of a significant anti-League minority on the board. However, Gray's opinions carried much weight as they were directed towards Dublin Castle. He condemned the Dingle guardians as 'a most scandalous board' and urged that the 'matter be brought under the notice of the Local Government Board'.[96] The Local Government Board had ultimate power over the guardians and it could dissolve any board and replace them with paid officials.[97] During the period of 1880–92, when Land and National League activists gained control of many board of guardians across the country, the Local Government Board issued official warnings and dissolved up to 13 unions. Hence, Gray's remarks, which were specifically aimed at the Local Government Board, whether substantially true or not had the potential to seriously undermine the National League-controlled board of guardians.

On Gray's advice, the chief secretary's office forwarded the reports on the Dingle board of guardians to the Local Government Board. Under the guidance of Sir Henry Robinson, it conceded that 'the meetings of the Guardian proceedings does not show that their meetings are irregularly or improperly performed', but it guaranteed that it would 'send [an] inspector unannounced to see how the board is run'.[98] Ominously for the Dingle board, Colonel Spaight, the inspector who had previously refused to sanction Patrick Ferriter's appointment as relieving officer carried out the investigation. In a damning report he stated that 'the Guardians are as a rule ignorant, uneducated and very un-businesslike and statements made by the sergeant of police [Moran] are substantially correct'.[99] Although Ferriter was in prison at the time of Spaight's inspection, the report claimed 'Ferriter guides the board as they are afraid to do anything without his consent.'[100] Two suggestions were now made to the Local Government Board to deal with the Dingle guardians: the chief secretary wondered 'whether raising the qualification rate [for entry to the board] would change the character of men',[101] while the RIC Divisional Inspector for the South West, Colonel Turner, called for its dissolution.[102] Both these measures were at the behest of the of the Local Government Board. This process depicts the willingness of the RIC and the Chief Secretary's Office to involve the Board in the political process of apprehending the National League.

By October 1888, the Local Government Board issued a warning against the Dingle board of guardians. It stated that the guardians 'have failed to carry out their obligations and brought a discreditable financial condition and unless there is an immediate improvement the union will be placed in other hands'.[103] Officially, the warning was issued on account of the board's failure to collect rates and because of hygiene concerns in the workhouse. Yet, the correspondence leading up to the warning between District Inspector Gray, the chief secretary's office and the Local Government Board focussed entirely on Ferriter's and the National League's influence over the Dingle guardians. Although the Local Government Board did warn and even dissolve unions due to their financial difficulties,[104] the non-collection of rates was a problem that had besieged the Dingle board for much of the decade and was prevalent before Lord Ventry lost his position as chairman in 1886. The unity of cohesive action between the RIC, the chief secretary's office, the Local Government Board and loyal guardians demonstrates the effective nature of the government's administration and its eagerness to manipulate every resource at its disposal to defeat the National League.

Despite the efforts of the authorities to undermine the nationalist guardians, the board remained a source of power for the National League. Resolutions passed by it were still of a nationalist nature and its patronage was extended to League activists. In early January 1889, the board condemned the arrest and imprisonment of Edward Harrington.[105] On another occasion, Lee was appointed as the board of guardians representative on the harbour board.[106] Nationalist activity also occurred outside the board. Reports of the local National League branches continued to appear in the *Kerry Sentinel*, although they largely dealt with broad national issues and did not resemble the 'League courts' of the past. In September 1888, the Parnell Indemnity Fund was established to finance the defence of Parnell and other nationalist MPs at the Special Commission. For the purpose of extending the Fund to Dingle, a public meeting was held in the town, which was attended by all the leading local National League activists, with Canon O'Sullivan in the chair, and Edward Harrington the principal speaker. Harrington contended that 'the people of Dingle may be very proud of the fight made by Patrick Ferriter' and paid tribute to region for the non-violent nature of agitation in the area,

> though there has been a little mixture of boycotting and what I call trinocheile [trouble] business ... I am glad of one fact that practically speaking there has hardly been a drop of bloodshed in this district during the whole agitation.[107]

He once again reiterated the guiding principles that dominated the Land League and the National League. He claimed that the people had a duty to 'look to themselves, to their wives, to their children and to those who they owe honest debts before any other claim [landlord's rent] is attended to' and declared, 'Do not grab land ... pledge yourselves that you shall never take a farm from which an honest man is evicted'.[108] Although the meeting had some of the hallmarks of earlier League gatherings, the organization remained seriously weakened. The crimes court was no longer held in the area – proof of a lack of coherent League activity – and boycotting levels continued to drop significantly, as did evictions: proof of a winding down of the land agitation that had dominated the region for the much of the decade.

While the National League became increasingly inactive, other nationalist organizations were established. By 1888, the Gaelic Athletic Association was rapidly expanding its structures throughout the country. A highly politicized body, it co-existed with the National League. A meeting of the suppressed Tralee National League was held at the pavilion under the stand during a Gaelic football match, thus spoiling police attempts at disrupting the illegal conclave.[109] As early as April 1888, Dublin Castle intelligence was of the impression that the 'GAA undoubtedly is now a far more dangerous association than the National League; it embraces the young and the old'.[110] However, the GAA was not fully extended to Kerry by this stage and was 'partially limited to Tralee, Listowel, Killarney and Castleisland'.[111] During the latter part of 1888, a coherent effort was made by nationalists to promote the organization in the county. Reports from the local clubs were published in the *Kerry Sentinel*. They resembled National League reports in structure, with committees established and resolutions proposed and adopted. Furthermore, the format of the reports in the *Kerry Sentinel* was identical with that of the League reports and they appeared alongside each other. In November, a county convention was held with delegates from the various regions of Kerry in attendance. The prominent National League organizer Michael Dissette represented Dingle, while members of the Castlegregory GAA also attended.[112] While the GAA did not become embroiled in the land agitation to the same extent as the National League, it was overtly political. At a football match involving Castlegregory, cheers were heard for William O'Brien and the Plan of Campaign.[113] The same branch christened itself the 'Allen' club after the Manchester Martyr, while the leading Tralee club was called 'John Mitchell's'.[114] When the second annual county convention was held, the GAA had expanded to Ballyferriter, Dingle and Castlegregory. The political nature of the GAA was expounded when it deemed,

> the objects of the association is [sic] to train young men in pastimes and unite to form an intercourse with other counties so as to unite in one network the whole of Ireland ... in addition to pastimes be a powerful auxiliary to the Irish national cause.[115]

Indeed, the GAA was to become one of the most powerful nationalist organizations in the country. Its emergence was part of the increasing nationalist fervour of the period, which on a local level largely grew out of the land agitation and the National League. There was clear National League involvement, in the formation of the GAA in Kerry – not only in the personnel involved but also through the application of the structures previously used to establish the League in the county. The device of the county convention and the use of the *Kerry Sentinel* to publicize the organization, were both factors that had been essential to the emergence of the League.

While the GAA's emergence provided nationalism with a new form of infrastructure and organization, the National League's last vestige of power in the Dingle region was its controlling position on the board of guardians. The run-up to the poor law elections of 1889 received (as usual) much press attention. The editorial of the *Kerry Sentinel* warned that 'in the Dingle Union the landlord factions are making strenuous exertions to regain their old supremacy'.[116] The newspaper's grievances proved well founded, as the National League candidates suffered severe losses. Although John Lee managed to get re-elected, albeit not in his old electoral division of Dingle but in Brandon, the National League representatives on the board were reduced to seven, leaving Lord Ventry with a large majority. As with the previous election in 1888, former National League activists switched allegiances on the new board. Both Terence O'Donnell, a large farmer elected to the Inch division and Maurice Nelligan (members of the League when it was at the height of its powers) voted for Lord Ventry, who was promptly elected chairman. Edward De Molyean, Ventry's land agent, was appointed vice-chairman, and Timothy Flaherty received the position of deputy vice-chairman, so the League lost all the controlling seats. This was a major defeat to the National League and signified the loss of its last powerful position in the Dingle region.

The victory of Lord Ventry signified the overall success of the government's policy in counteracting the National League in the region. The suppression of the organization followed by the stringent implementation of the Crimes Act by the police and the judiciary deprived the League of its 'court system' and the ability to enforce boycotting. Although resistance to the suppression of the League emerged, most notably through the activities of Patrick Ferriter, the Crimes Act had its intended effect with boycotting levels and the overall potency of the League drastically reduced. The infrastructure of the League, founded in its regular meetings, was seriously disrupted by police intervention; eventually reports of meetings appeared in the press that were often fictional and 'bogus'. These factors coupled with the more favourably terms bestowed on the tenantry by the land legislation of the period led to the end of National League-orchestrated agrarian agitation. Inevitably, this was to have serious implications for the League-controlled board of guardians. Deprived of the organizational and influential strength that had guaranteed it electoral success in the past, it suffered serious losses at poor law elections. As the National League weakened, former activists quickly affirmed their loyalty to Lord Ventry; this could be seen in the increasing number of anti-League guardians on the poor law board. The dwindling power of the League in relation to the board of guardians was augmented by a systematic government effort to remove the nationalist guardians. The constabulary, chief secretary's office and Local Government Board acted in a highly organized and cohesive manner against the National League-controlled board of guardians. The incorporation of the Local Government Board into the overall process of defeating the National League on a local level further depicts the politicization of that body. By the turn of the decade, the National League was a defunct organization in the region.

By the time Lord Ventry had recaptured the Dingle board of guardians in April 1889, land agitation nationwide was at extremely low ebb. During the height of the agitation, politics were fought at a local level. Activists challenged the power of the landlord class and the government authorities through the infrastructure of the Land and National Leagues. However, the suppression of the National League and the winding down of the land war throughout the country led to a decline in activity at local level. Although not every National League branch countrywide was suppressed, fear of the Crimes Act led to inactivity and many local League branches became dormant. The ailing 'Plan of Campaign' remained the sole outlet for agrarian agitation during the late 1880s. Actuated on less than 1 per cent of the estates in Ireland, it was nowhere as deeply rooted as the National or Land Leagues had been and it was seriously undermined by Parnell's refusal to be associated with it and his determination to focus on home rule.[117] Plagued by lack of total support from the Irish Parliamentary Party and a crippling financial situation, the 'Plan' was facing total failure.

In response to this situation, the Tenants Defence Association was established in late 1889. It received the backing of the Parliamentary Party and, most importantly, Parnell. Although officially a measure created in response to increasingly stringent landlord syndicates, it was essentially a financial rescue operation for the beleaguered 'Plan'.[118] Under the Tenants Defence Association's constitution, no branches were to be established but county conventions and local meetings were to be held for the purpose of creating a fund to 'provide legal advice, support and financial support for evicted tenants'.[119] Furthermore, Timothy Harrington privately stated it was an opportunity 'to demonstrate the strength of the organisation of the National League'.[120] Leading members of the Parliamentary Party aligned themselves closely with the movement, this creating the impression that the party was identifying itself more closely with the agrarian agitation than it had done for several years. County conventions were staged countrywide with large-scale involvement by local National League branches. The Kerry convention held in late November 1889 was attended by representatives from across the Dingle region including National League leaders Lee and Ferriter.[121] The Tenants Defence Association in effect infused new life into the 'Plan of Campaign' and the branch structure of the National League. However, the agitation remained within the confines of the 'Plan' estates, and the local National League branches did not regain their former strength.

With a renewed vigour in agrarian agitation and Parnell's position strengthened by the collapse of the prosecutions case at the Special Commission, Irish nationalism was on an upward trend during late 1889–90. Yet, the movement was to become bitterly divided and left in tatters after the Parnell split. After the divorce case of Kitty O'Shea from Captain O'Shea, with Parnell cited as a co-respondent, nationalist Ireland was rendered into pro- and anti-Parnell camps. Although Parnell maintained control of the structure of the National League, the anti-Parnellite majority seceded from it and formed the Irish National Federation led by Justin McCarthy with the support of John Dillon, William O'Brien and Timothy Healy.[122] Local branches emerged throughout the country acting in opposition to the National League. Once again, the emphasis refocused on local politics as campaigners from both sides turned to the people for support. Like the rest of the country, former allies descended into bitter rivalry in Kerry. Out of the four MPs in the county, three (J.D. Sheehan, Denis Kilbride, Thomas Sexton) supported the anti-Parnellites, while Edward Harrington remained loyal to Parnell. The *Kerry Sentinel* staunchly supported Parnell during the split and refused to report on the activities of the Irish National Federation. Despite the anti-Parnellites being deprived of the main nationalists media voice in the county, the Federation had the substantial support of the clergy. In January 1891, 67 priests from all around the county signed a protest against Parnell's leadership. Notably, Canon O'Sullivan, the leading clerical figure in the National League in the Dingle region, declined to sign it.[123] Despite this, local clergy played a major role in organizing the Federation in Dingle and throughout the region. When Sheehan and Kilbride toured Castlegregory and Dingle to extend the

Federation to the region, it was the clergy they met and the clergy chaired the meetings. In Castlegregory, Fr Molyneaux, a founding member of the National League in the area, greeted the anti-Parnellites, while in Dingle the local clergy turned out in force, led largely by Fr Scollard.[124] In response, a delegation from Tralee comprising of Edward Harrington and Michael Dissette (by this stage a prominent Parnellite in Tralee) arrived in Dingle to promote Parnell at a meeting attended by hardened League activists such as Lee and Ferriter.[125] Despite the canvassing of the pro-Parnellites, the power and influence of the clergy was to prove too much. The local clergy vehemently pursed the anti-Parnellite agenda with Scollard preaching in sermons in the Dingle area that 'all following Mr Parnell are guilty of breaking both the second and sixth commandment'.[126] However, the lack of sources means it is not possible to provide details about the split in the Dingle region. Although the poor law elections in 1891 were fought along pro- and anti-Parnellite lines in some areas of the county, little or no coverage was provided in the newspapers for the proceedings in the Dingle region. The *Kerry Sentinel* merely declared that Lord Ventry was elected unanimously.[127] In the Tralee poor law union, an area that was Edward Harrington's stronghold and where the board of guardians had been a traditional source of power for local Leaguers, the election was bitterly contested. Significantly the anti-Parnellites gained control of the board indicating the lack of popular support for Parnell and his supporters in the town.[128] The Federation was to be uniformly successful in defeating the pro-Parnellites and National League. In the general election of 1892, all the MPs returned for Kerry were anti-Parnellite, with Edward Harrington losing his West Kerry seat to Sir Thomas Gratton. A landlord from Wexford, Gratton was a strong supporter of Tim Healy who had married the daughter of a wealthy Tralee merchant, Sir Henry Donovan.[129] In the aftermath of the division that racked nationalism in Ireland, the National League and the 'Plan of Campaign' disintegrated, marking an end to the agitation that had dominated the previous decade. Within the Dingle region, Lord Ventry remained chairman of the board of guardians for the rest of the 1890s.

Conclusion

By 1892 the National League was a defunct organization in the Dingle region. When it originally emerged in the area in 1885 it acted as a more sophisticated, organized and united movement than the previous Land Leagues. Its network of branches located across the Dingle peninsula provided it with a coherent and powerful infrastructure. In the general election of 1885 the National League on a local level provided Parnell with his strongest hand in the house of commons as it acted as an electioneering machine that ensured the successful return of nationalist candidates. While the attainment of home rule was the primary factor driving the national leadership of the League, the land agitation inevitably dominated the movement at a local level. Branches paid lip-service to home rule by passing resolutions supporting it, yet little real debate took place on the issue. As the National League expanded in Dingle and the county generally, the land agitation was accelerated. The League orchestrated non-payment of rents and offered protection to tenants. Central to League policy was to undermine the landlord position by making evictions untenable by preventing tenants from taking evicted farms or what was known as 'land-grabbing'. Branch meetings quickly came to resemble 'courts', with offenders, witnesses and the presentation of evidence dominating proceedings as the National League tried offenders according to its rules. Those who were found to have breached its regulations were subjected to punishment. While the National League fined and expelled offenders from the organization, its most powerful weapon was undoubtedly the boycott, a form of stringent social and economic ostracism that few in society could withstand. Through the infrastructure of the branch system that revolved around weekly meetings and the power of the boycott, the National League came to the forefront of society in the Dingle region as it successfully enforced its regulations and edicts. The 'League courts' replaced the authority previously held by the government authorities to the stage where they held more power than the RIC.

As the power of the National League intensified, it began to regulate aspects of society outside the landlord-tenant conflict. Agricultural labourers were involved in the organization to the extent that the League passed resolutions in their favour at the expense of tenant farmers, particularly in relation to the setting of conacre rents. Other economic groups, such as carriers in Dingle town, lobbied through the structures of the League to gain cartage employment. These instances demonstrate that, as the League broadened its remit, the character of the organization began to resemble the structure and tensions of the surrounding rural society on which it attempted to stamp its own economic and social policies. Also, the involvement of the National League in issues beyond the agrarian agitation, between landlord and tenant, reflected its increased authority. This was extended to the most powerful institute in local government and politics in the area, the board of guardians. Traditionally a source of power for Lord Ventry, National League backed candidates overwhelmingly defeated the 'loyal' guardians during the poor law elections of March 1886. Less than a year after its inception in the Dingle region, the League had dramatically come to the forefront of society. Its 'courts' not only regulated landlord-tenant relations but also the economic relationship between the farming community and various groups within society such as agricultural labourers and carriers. Also League power was extended to the local government of the time, the board of guardians. In *realpolitic* the League was the authority in the region. Furthermore, while boycotting provided the basis of its power, it rarely resorted to the violence that marked the agitation in other localities.

However, tensions and divisions came to rack the movement as the effects of boycotting caused internal dissension. The Dingle and Ballyferriter branches descended into open conflict over the issuing of boycotts. Constant complaints were lodged at the central branch of the National League over the abusive enactment of boycotting leading to the dissolution of the Dingle branch. At the heart of these incidents were class divisions between farmers and traders and political issues arousing from constitutional and more radical forces within the movement. They underlined the divisions that were inherent in the movement both socially and politically. Although the structure and strength of the League were undermined, it continued in its past vigour. The 'Ballyferriter evictions' depicted the National League's organizational ability as it successfully prevented the eviction of tenants in the face of large government forces in early 1887. However, the National League was to be seriously weakened following the appointment of Arthur Balfour as chief secretary. His Crimes Act in the latter half of 1887 led to suppression the National League in the Dingle region. The Dingle RIC under the leadership of District Inspector Gray, aided by the judiciary, rigorously implemented the provisions of the coercive laws. Deprived of its weekly meetings, the National League structure lay in ruins. League reports in the *Kerry Sentinel* were often deemed to be fictional and bogus. Boycotting levels dropped to the stage where in April 1888 it was reported to be non-existent. Land legislation favourable to tenants further dampened the agitation that had dominated the 1885–87 period in Dingle. The National League's position as the dominant authority in the locality rapidly disintegrated. It maintained its controlling position on the board of guardians, yet this became the target of intense pressure. The constabulary, the chief secretary's office and the Local Government Board all acted in a cohesive manner to dislodge the League guardians. In March 1889 the National League's loss of power was complete when Lord Ventry was re-elected as chairman of the board. The National League and the nationalist movement was ravaged and bitterly torn apart by the Parnell split. The National Federation was established as a counter organisation against the National League bringing to an end the agrarian agitation.

Notes

ABBREVIATIONS

CBS	Crime Branch Special
CSO	Chief Secretary's Office
CSO RP	Chief Secretary's Office Register Papers
GAA	Gaelic Athletic Association
KS	*Kerry Sentinel*
KEP	*Kerry Evening Post*
NAI	National Archives Ireland
NLI	National Library of Ireland
NLLB	National League Letter Book
RIC	Royal Irish Constabularly

INTRODUCTION

1 *Landowners in Ireland, 1876* (Baltimore, 1988), p. 145.
2 J. Lee, *The modernisation of Irish society, 1848–1918* (Dublin, 1973), p. 80.
3 Lee, *Modernisation*, p. 82.
4 T. O'Sullivan, *Romantic hidden Kerry* (Kerry, 1931), p. 246.
5 S.A. Bell, 'Policing the land war: official responses to political protest and agrarian crime in Ireland, 1879–91' (unpublished Ph.D. thesis, Goldsmith's College, University of London, 2000) p. 239.
6 Lee, *Modernisation*, p. 81.
7 *Special Commission act, reprint of the shorthand notes of the speeches, proceedings and evidence taken before the commissioners appointed under the above act* (8 vols, London, 1890), p. 488.
8 *Special Commission act, reprint*, viii, p. 488.
9 M. O'Callaghan, *British high politics and a nationalist Ireland: criminality, land and the law under Forster and Balfour* (Cork, 1994), p. 114.
10 Virginia Crossman, *Politics, law and order in nineteenth-century Ireland* (Dublin, 1996), p. 148.
11 NLI, National League Letter Book 1883–1886.
12 *Report of the royal commission on the Land Law (Ireland) Act, 1881, and Purchase of Land (Ireland) Act, 1885*, [4969], H.C. 1887, xxvi, vol. ii: Minutes of evidence and appendices, p. 555
13 O'Sullivan, *Kerry*.
14 O'Callaghan, *British high politics*.
15 Donald Jordan, 'The Irish National League and the "unwritten law": rural protest and nation building in Ireland' in *Past & Present*, 158 (Feb. 1998).
16 J.S. Donnelly, *The land and the people of nineteenth-century Cork: the rural economy and the Land Question* (London, 1975) and 'Kenmare estates in the nineteenth century' in *Journal of the Kerry Archaeological and Historical Society* xxiii (1993).
17 W. Feingold, *The revolt of the tenantry: the transformation of local government in Ireland, 1872–86* (Boston, 1984).
18 V. Crossman, *Local government in nineteenth-century Ireland* (Belfast, 1994), p. 53.

1. THE ESTABLISHMENT OF THE IRISH NATIONAL LEAGUE IN THE DINGLE POOR LAW UNION

1 Crossman, *Local government*, p. 50.
2 W.L. Feingold, 'The tenants' movement to capture the Irish Poor Law boards, 1877–86' in *Albion*, viii (1975) 219.
3 Crossman, *Local government*, p. 45.
4 W.F. Bailey, *Local and centralised government in Ireland: a sketch of the existing systems* (1888), p. 29.
5 Feingold, *The revolt of the tenantry* p. 19.
6 Feingold, 'The tenants' movement', p. 217.
7 Ibid. p. 224.
8 Bailey, *Local and centralised*, p. 27.
9 *Guy's postal directory of Munster, 1886* (1886), p. 416.
10 Bailey, *Local and centralised*, p. 26.
11 *Guy's postal directory*, p. 416.
12 *Landowners in Ireland, 1876* (Baltimore, 1988), pp 141–5.
13 *The agricultural statistics for Ireland for the year 1881, [3332]*, H.C. 1882, lxxiv, p. 19.
14 Ibid., p. 31.
15 Ibid.
16 O'Callaghan, *British high politics*, p. 106.
17 T. Barrington, 'A review of Irish agricultural prices' in *Journal of the Statistical and Social Inquiry Society of Ireland*, xv (1927) 252.
18 NAI, CSO, Irish Land and National League Papers, Carton 7.
19 *Kerry Sentinel*, 7 May 1885.
20 Ibid.
21 Ibid.
22 *Guy's postal directory of Munster, 1886*, p. 417. In *Guy's* the largest farmers in each area were categorized as 'prominent' farmers; no acreage for these farmers was stated. *K.S*, 7 May 1885.
23 P. Bew, *Charles Stewart Parnell* (2nd ed., Dublin, 1991), p. 63.
24 O'Sullivan, *Kerry* p. 258.
25 KS, 25 Sept 1885.
26 O'Sullivan, *Kerry*, p. 259 KS, 20 Nov 1885.
27 KS, 8 May 1885 KS, 24 April 1885.
28 KS, 20 Nov. 1885.
29 *Guy's postal directory*, p. 417.
30 KS, 30 Oct. 1885. The constituency of West Kerry had a population of 45,964 and comprised the Dingle poor law union and other areas including Tralee and Killorglin. For size, population and election results for the constituency, see B.M. Walker (ed.), *Parliamentary election results in Ireland, 1801–1922* (Dublin, 1978), p. 353.
31 O'Sullivan, *Kerry*, p. 260.
32 KS, 20 Nov 1885.
33 *Kerry Evening Post*, 5 Aug 1885.
34 Ibid.
35 *KEP*, 21 Nov. 1885.
36 KS, 27 Nov. 1885.
37 P. Foley, *History of the natural, civil, military and ecclesiastical state of county Kerry: Corkaguiny* (Dublin, 1907), p. 162.
38 KS, 24 Apr. 1885.
39 KS, 18 May 1885.
40 Harrington to Fr Gilchirst, NLI, National League Letter Book 1883–88, no. 24
41 NAI, CSO RP, 1886, box 3310, 1887.
42 Bell, 'Policing the Land War'; p. 229.
43 D. Jordan, 'The Irish National League', p. 162.
44 Ibid., p. 163.
45 KS, 25 Nov. 1885.
46 KS, 26 Feb. 1886.
47 *Special Commission Act, 1888*, ii, p. 460.
48 Bell, 'Policing the Land War', p. 246.
49 *Special Commission Act, 1888*, ii, p. 460.
50 *Guy's postal directory*, p. 416. *Report of the royal commission on the Land Law (Ireland) Act, 1881, and Purchase of Land (Ireland) Act, 1885*, [4969], H.C. 1887, xxvi, vol. ii: Minutes of evidence and appendices, p. 555 (hereafter *Cowper commission*).
51 Ibid.
52 KS, 22 June 1886.
53 *Cowper commission*, evidence, p. 555.
54 NAI, Chief Secretary Office Registered Papers, Jan 1886, box 3310/ 1887.
55 *Cowper Commission*, evidence, p. 555.
56 Ibid.
57 Ibid.
58 Emergency men were employed to work on evicted farms that were boycotted. They were often supplied by landlord associations set up to counter the effects of boycotting such as the Land Corporation and the Cork Defence Union.

59 Foley, *Corkaguiny*, p. 263.
60 NAI, CSO RP, July 1886, box 3310/1887.
61 Ibid., *K.S.*, 28 Feb 1886.
62 NAI, CSO RP, Jan 1886, box 3310/1887.
63 Ibid.
64 Ibid.
65 *Cowper commission,* evidence, pp 383.
66 Ibid.

2. THE GROWTH OF THE LEAGUE

1 Jordan, 'The Irish National League' p. 162.
2 Bell, 'Policing the Land War'
3 CSO, Irish Land League and National League papers, carton 7, half yearly report on National League 1 Jan–30 June 1885.
4 O'Callaghan, *British high politics* p. 113.
5 NAI, CSO RP, July 1886, box 3310/1887.
6 NAI, CSO RP, Jan 1886, box 3310/1887.
7 Ibid.
8 Ibid.
9 *Special Commission Act, 1888*, ii, p. 499.
10 NAI, CSO RP, Jan 1886, box 3302/1887.
11 *Special Commission Act, 1888,* ii, p 16.
12 Ibid.
13 *KS*, 12 March 1886.
14 *KS*, 12 February 1886.
15 *KS*, 21 February 1886.
16 J.S. Donnelly, *The land and the people* p. 324.
17 Jordan, 'The Irish National League' p. 153.
18 L.M. Geary, *The Plan of Campaign, 1886–91* (Cork, 1986), p. 11.
19 NAI, CSORP, April 1886, box 3310/1887.
20 For example, see J.S. Donnelly, 'Kenmare estates' p. 9.
21 J.S. Donnelly, p. 319.
22 For example, see *KS*, 23 Nov 1886.
23 *KS*, 5 July 1886.
24 NAI, CSORP, June 1886, box 3310/1887.
25 *KS*, 18 July 1886.
26 *Guy's postal directory*, p. 417.
27 *KS,* 5 Nov 1886.
28 *Guy's postal directory*, p. 109.
29 D. Fitzpatrick, 'The disappearance of the Irish agricultural labourer, 1841–1911' in *Irish Economic and Social History* vii (1980) 84.
30 Donnelly, *The land and the people* p. 242.
31 P.L.R. Horn, 'The national agricultural labourers union in Ireland 1873–9' in *IHS*, xvii (1971), 42.
32 K.T. Hoppen, *Elections politics and society in Ireland, 1832–85* (Oxford, 1984), p. 475.
33 S. Clark, *Social origins of the Irish land war* (Princeton, 1979), p. 15.
34 P. Bew, *Land and the national question in Ireland, 1858–82* (Dublin, 1978), p. 174.
35 *KS*, 25 May 1885.
36 Hoppen, *Elections*, p. 478.
37 For example, see *KEP*, 13 June 1885 and 29 July 1885.
38 *KS*, 29 Feb 1886.
39 *KS*, 5 July 1886.
40 *KS*, 29 June 1886.
41 *KS*, 5 July 1886.
42 *KS*, 4 Feb 1887.
43 *KS*, 23 July 1886.
44 *KS*, 8 May 1886.
45 W.L. Feingold, *The Irish boards of poor law guardians, 1872–86, a revolution in local government* (Chicago, 1974), p. 87.
46 *Thom's Official Directory of the United Kingdom and Ireland for the year 1886* (1886), p. 1090.
47 Foley, *Corkaguiny*, p. 275.
48 *KS*, 26 March 1886.
49 Minutes of Dingle board of guardians, 1 April 1886. Kerry County Library.
50 KS, 9 Feb 1886.
51 Ibid.
52 Ibid., 16 March 1886.
53 Ibid., 20 June 1886. .
54 For example, see, *KEP*, 2 June 1886.
55 W. F. Bailey, *Local and centralised* p. 26.
56 *Return of the boards of poor law guardians in Ireland dissolved or warned by Local Government Board, 1880–90*, H.C. 1892, lxviii, 965.
57 Appeared on platform of loyalist meeting in Cork, *KEP*, 31 March 1886.
58 Minutes of Dingle board of guardians, 15 April 1886.
59 *KEP*, 9 June 1886.
60 Foley, *Corkaguiny*, pp 286.
61 Minutes of Dingle board of guardians, 18 Dec 1886.
62 *KS*, 28 Jan 1886.

3. DECLINE AND FALL OF THE LEAGUE

1 Harrington to Gilchirst, NLI, National League Letter Book 1883–88, no 24. Geary, *The Plan of Campaign* p. 12.
2 NAI, CSO RP, Jan 1886, box 3310/1887.
3 Harrington to Ferriter, NLI, NLLB 1883–8, no 76.
4 *KS*, 21 May 1886.
5 Murphy to Harrington, 7 June 1886, NLI, Harrington papers MS 8933[5].
6 Ibid.
7 Ibid.
8 Harrington to Ferriter, NLI, NLLB 1883–8, no 86.
9 *KS*, 10 Aug. 1886.
10 Murphy to Harrington, 20 July 1886, NLI, Harrington papers MS 8933[5].
11 *KS*, 16 July 1886.
12 *Slater's directory 1881*.
13 Harrington to Murphy, NLI, NLLB 1883–8, no 93.
14 Ibid.
15 Murphy to Harrington, 30 Aug. 1886, NLI, Harrington papers, Ms 8933[5].
16 Harrington to Murphy, 1 Sept 1886, NLI, NLLB 1883–8, no 104.
17 Harrington to Kelliher, 30 Sept. 1886, NLI, NLLB 1883–8, no 106.
18 Murphy to Harrington, 30 Aug. 1886, NLI, Harrington papers, Ms 8933[5].
19 Murphy to Harrington, 20 July 1886, NLI, Harrington Papers Ms 8933[5].
20 *KEP*, 11 Sept 1886.
21 Ferriter to Harrington, 14 Sept 1886, NLI, Harrington papers MS 8933[5].
22 Harrington to Fr Scully, 6 Oct 1886, NLI, NLLB, no 106.
23 Harrington to McCarthy, 8 Mar. 1887, NLI, NLLB, no 127.
24 *KEP*, 9 July 1887.
25 Crossman, *Politics*, p. 157.
26 Geary, *The Plan of Campaign* p. 180.
27 *KS*, 27 Jan. 1887.
28 NAI, CSO RP, Jan. 1887, box 3310/1887.
29 Geary, *The Plan of Campaign*, p. 26.
30 NAI, CSO RP, Jan. 1887, box 3310/1887.
31 Foley, *Corkaguiny*, p. 281.
32 *KEP*, 19 Feb 1887
33 Ibid.
34 Ibid.
35 Crossman, *Politics*, p. 158.
36 For a comprehensive comment on General Buller in Ireland see, O'Callaghan, *British high politics*, pp 132–44.
37 C. P. Crane, *Memories of a resident magistrate, 1880–1920* (Edinburgh, 1938), p. 105.
38 Ibid.
39 *KEP*, 23 Feb 1887.
40 Ibid.
41 *KS*, 1 March 1887.
42 Ibid.
43 *KEP*, 16 April 1887.
44 Geary, *Plan of Campaign*, p.179.
45 NAI, CSO CBS, Divisional Commissioners and County Inspectors reports, South Western Division 1887–98, carton 4, April 1887.
46 Crossman, *Politics*, p.162.
47 NAI, CSO CBS, Divisional Commissioners and County Inspectors reports, carton 4 June 1887.
48 *KS*, 3 June 1887.
49 *KEP*, 23 July 1887.
50 NAI, CSO CBS, Divisional Commissioners and County Inspectors reports, carton 4, August, 1887,
51 *KEP*, 10 August 1887.
52 Bell, 'Policing the Land War:' p. 264.
53 L.P. Curtis, *Coercion and conciliation in Ireland* (London, 1963), p. 218.
54 NAI, CSO CBS, Divisional Commissioner's and County Inspector's reports, carton 4, August 1887.
55 P. Foley, *Corkaguiny*, p. 291.
56 Bell, 'Policing the Land War,' p. 265.
57 NAI, CSO CBS, Divisional Commissioner's and County Inspector's reports, carton 4, November 1887.
58 Ibid.
59 Ibid.
60 Ibid.
61 *KS*, 18 Oct. 1887.
62 Between August 1887 and March 1888 Roche RM heard cases involving ninety people in which 84 were prosecuted mostly in the Kerry region; see for list of number of convictions given by each in the country for this period, T. Harrington, *A diary of coercion being a list of the cases tried under the Criminal Law and Procedure Act: part I* (Dublin, 1888), preface.

63 *KS*, 25 Jan 1888.
64 Harrington, *A diary of coercion: part I*, p. 55. This work is a list and description of prosecutions under the aforementioned Act published by Timothy Harrington as a result of Balfour the chief secretary refusing to issue a parliamentary return of cases tried under the act.
65 *KS*, 21 March 1888.
66 *KS*, 4 Nov. 1887.
67 *KEP*, 2 Nov. 1887.
68 *KEP*, 3 Dec. 1887.
69 *KEP*, 25 Dec 1887.
70 *KS*, 20 Apr. 1888.
71 T. Harrington, *A diary of coercion part II* (Dublin, 1888), p. 37.
72 *KEP*, 25 April 1888.
73 NAI, CSO Divisional, January 1888, Carton 4.
74 *KS*, 25 Apr. 1888.
75 *KS*, 25 Apr. 1888.
76 NAI, CSO Irish Land and National League papers, box 7, 1 July–30 Sep 1887.
77 Curtis, *Coercion*, p. 220.
78 Donnelly, *The land and the people* p. 373.
79 *KEP*, 19 Jan 1889.
80 NAI, CSO RP, Aug. 1888, box 3421/1888.
81 *KEP*, 28 Mar. 1888.
82 *KS*, 26 Mar. 1888.
83 *KS*, 26 Mar. 1886, see also chp 2 p.
84 *Guy's postal directory*, p. 223. Fitzgerald was from the parish of Drom in the Cloghane electoral division
85 *Guy's postal directory* p. 109. Long was from the parish of Ballyaglisha in the Dunurlin electoral division and was a guardian since the emergence of the National League.
86 *KS*, 5 May 1885.
87 Received letters from Harrington on 11 Dec. 1886, see Timothy Harrington's National League letter book, 1883–88, INL, INLLB letter 113. Also see Harrington Papers ms 8933(5).
88 *KS*, 11 June 1887.
89 Minutes of Dingle board of guardians, 9 Feb. 1889, Kerry County Library.
90 NAI, CSO Divisional Commissioners and County Inspectors reports, carton 4, Aug 1887.
91 Ibid., November 1887.
92 *KS*, 4 Apr. 1889.
93 NAI, CSO RP, 14 April 1888, 18272/1888.
94 Ibid.
95 Ibid.
96 NAI, CSO RP, 14 Apr. 1888, box 3241/1888.
97 W.L. Feingold, *The revolt of the tenantry: the transformation of local government in Ireland, 1872–86* (Boston, 1984), p. 17.
98 NAI, CSO RP, 21 April 1888, 18272/1888.
99 NAI, CSO RP, 3 July 1888, 18272/1888.
100 Ibid.
101 NAI, CSO RP, 3 July 1888, 18272/1888.
102 NAI, CSO RP, 20 July 1888, 18272/1888.
103 KEP, 6 Oct 1888.
104 *Annual report of the Local Government Board for Ireland being the sixteenth report of the Local Government Board (Ireland) Act*, p. 80. Ballyvaghan Union dissolved for the inadequate financial position of the board.
105 *KS*, 13 Jan 1889.
106 *KS*, 22 Dec 1888.
107 *KS*, 29 Sep 1888.
108 Ibid.
109 *KS*, 28 March 1888.
110 NAI, CBS, Divisional Commissioners and County Inspectors reports, carton 4, 4 April 1888.
111 NAI, CBS, Divisional Commissioners and County Inspectors reports, carton 4, 5 March 1888.
112 *KS*, 10 Nov 1888.
113 *KS*, 10 April 1888.
114 *KS*, 15 June 1888.
115 *KS*, 28 Oct 1889.
116 *KS*, 3 April 1889.
117 For a comprehensive analysis of Parnell's often acrimonious relationship with the 'Plan of Campaign' see, L.M. Geary, *The Plan of Campaign* (Cork, 1986).
118 Geary, *The Plan of Campaign*, p. 126.
119 Thomas Bradley Papers Ms 33,561/(4), NLI.
120 Thomas Bradley Papers Ms 33,561/6), NLI.
121 *KS*, 20 Nov 1889.
122 Frank Callanan, *The Parnell split, 1890–91*, (Cork, 1992), p. 110.

123 Thomas O'Sullivan, *Romantic hidden Kerry: a description of Corkaguiny* (Tralee, 1934), p. 283.
124 *Cork Examiner*, 2 March 1890.
125 *KS*, 2 Mar. 1890.
126 *KS*, 4 Apr. 1890.
127 *KS*, 8 Apr. 1890.
128 *KS*, 8 Apr. 1890.
129 J.A Gaughan, *A political odyssey: Thomas O'Donnell, M.P. for West Kerry 1900–1918* (Kildare, 1983) p. 42.